Toddlers Gone Wild!

rants from a **mommy** brain

Rebecca Eckler

KEY PORTER BOOKS

Library and Archives Canada Cataloguing in Publication

Eckler, Rebecca
Toddlers gone wild! / Rebecca Eckler.

ISBN 978-1-55263-987-0

1. Toddlers—Humor. 2. Parenting—Humor. 3. Mothers—Humor.
I. Title.

HQ759.E228 2008   649'.1220207   C2007-905452-8

ONTARIO ARTS COUNCIL
CONSEIL DES ARTS DE L'ONTARIO

The publisher gratefully acknowledges the support of the Canada Council for the Arts
and the Ontario Arts Council for its publishing program. We acknowledge the support of the Government of Ontario through the Ontario Media Development
Corporation's Ontario Book Initiative.

We acknowledge the financial support of the Government of Canada through the
Book Publishing Industry Development Program (BPIDP) for our publishing activities.

Key Porter Books Limited
Six Adelaide Street East, Tenth Floor
Toronto, Ontario
Canada M5C 1H6

www.keyporter.com

Text design: Marijke Friesen
Electronic formatting: Alison Carr

Printed and bound in Canada

08 09 10 11 12 5 4 3 2 1

Rebecca, Jasmine, Victoria and Joanna—
the best friends a gal could ask for.
And, of course, Rowan Joely, my heart.

A Note from the Author

I can't ever seem to please my "boss."

I'm her chef, chauffeur, stylist, personal shopper, teacher, housekeeper and confidant. I even prepare her baths so the temperature is just right. Simply put, I do everything for her.

But, this morning, the microwavable pancakes I prepared are not hot enough (I'm sorry, microwaving is a form of cooking, as is "take-out"). There's not enough butter. The apple juice is too cold. She doesn't want Elmo. She wants Curious George. She wants a blanket. But not *that* blanket. The pink one! No, not *that* pink one! The other one. No, not that one either! Oh, she wants the pink one that is actually not pink at all. It's blue!

My "boss" is in full-blown diva mode this morning.

If "my boss" wasn't my *daughter* this would be the point at which I'd look her squarely in the eye and say, "I quit!"

But she is my daughter. And she's only 4. And it's 7:30 in the morning and we have to be out the door in half an hour to get her to junior kindergarten so she can color all day, and, if she's lucky, I guess, paint. And maybe learn something.

This morning, when the alarm went off, I rolled over my daughter to hit the snooze button. (Yes, my "boss" was in my bed. Are you surprised?)

"Mommy, I want to sleep for four more hours," she said.

"Okay," I mumbled, dozing off. I hadn't slept so well, what with her 4-year-old legs kicking me and her arms around my neck for most of the night. We also slept with Clancy, her stuffed bear who is the size of a bar fridge.

Eventually, I forced myself out of bed. I am responsible now. I am the mother of a toddler, and part of being responsible for a toddler is making sure that she—my boss—gets to junior kindergarten on time. I can't have my toddler exhibiting "truancy" problems just yet. She can't be a pre-school drop out.

Still, if I don't say, "Eat!" every 2.5 seconds—so we can then get dressed and brush her hair and teeth—we won't be getting out of the door until Thursday. It's Monday.

It looks like I'll be dropping her off at school in my pajamas—again.

Oh, how my life has changed! And not because I don't really have one—a life, that is—anymore. Only four years ago, my "boss" was in my tummy. I chronicled the experience of being unexpectedly expecting in *Knocked Up: Confessions of a Hip Mother-to-Be*. I chronicled the first two years of motherhood in *Wiped! Life with a Pint-size Dictator*.

But, oh, the boddler years (those years when your child is no longer a baby, but not quite a toddler)! Oh, how many times have I wiped her nose on my sleeve because there are never tissues around when you need them? Oh, how many times have I somehow managed to live through her meltdowns? Oh, how many times have I been to birthday parties and eaten sugary cake and tried to make small talk with other parents—most of whom seem to have their shit together way more than I do? Oh, how many times I have let my toddler leave the house looking like a Christmas tree? Oh, how many times have I wiped her ass?

Toddlers Gone Wild is a collection of essays—you could call them rants from a mommy brain—that explores the ups and downs, the ins and outs of these crazy, hectic, chaotic, sleep-deprived years. (I haven't had a solid eight-hour sleep since. . . . What year is it?) This is not an advice book. Aside from raising a boddler/toddler, what do I know? (Except that it doesn't help to cry when your toddler is having a temper tantrum and no matter how "careful" your toddler tells you she'll be, it's never a good idea to let her eat an ice cream cone in the car.)

These mini-monologues are meant to be self-deprecating. Hopefully all you wonderful mothers and mothers-to-be can sympathize. This time in our lives doesn't last forever, after all. It only seems like it does.

Oh, back to this morning. Just as we managed to get out the door (after only fifty-four bribes), my toddler looked at me and said, "Mommy, you're the best mommy in the world."

Maybe we should want the toddler years to last forever after all.

—Rebecca Eckler
Toronto, 2008

Part I
What's Happened to Me?

Matt: Mommy, I have a new name for you.
Mommy: What is it?
Matt: Super Mommy
Mommy: I love that name. You can always call me that.
Matt: You're my best friend, Super Mommy!

Matt, 3, son of Laural Adams

The Ass Is Always Greener

Your life has changed drastically since becoming a mother. You thought you would get some semblance of your pre-baby life back as your baby turned into a toddler. This may be true. But some things never go back.

I was one of those women who thought that my body would bounce right back after I gave birth. How could I not think that in this day and age?

First of all, everyone told me it would. Everyone told me not to worry. Everyone was all, like, "Don't worry, your body will bounce back!" Which, when you're pregnant, is the equivalent of going through a breakup and having your friends tell you, "Of course you're not going to be alone forever. Of course you'll find someone else."

It turns out that friends don't always tell you the truth. My body *so* did not bounce back. Thanks to celebrities, I honestly (and naively) thought that I'd get my pre-pregnancy body back three weeks after giving birth. Of course, the celebrities probably all exercised during their pregnancies and didn't eat four Big Macs a week like I had. My cravings for chocolate and Big Macs didn't go away after I gave birth. They still haven't.

After about six months of hard exercise and eating as well as I could, I did fit into my pre-pregnancy clothes again. But I'm telling you, fitting into your pre-pregnancy clothes is not the same as getting your pre-pregnancy body back. Oh, no, no, no.

I could talk about doing shoulder stands in yoga and seeing the skin flap around my navel, like the skin of an elephant. My yoga friend, also a mother, has the same problem. But no one really sees you in a shoulder-stand position anyway, except you.

Everyone, however, sees your butt.

My ass has not been the same since I got pregnant. I have body parts that I'm not proud of—my nose, my oh-so-pointy elbows, my weak chin. I could go on, but I really just want to complain about my ass.

Pre-pregnancy, I was doing about three or four spin classes a week. My ass was tight and hard and small. I wasn't aware of it at the time, but I should have been. It's like looking at photos of yourself when you were 16 and seeing that you were covering your stomach. You think, "Why was I covering my stomach then?"

About a month ago, I walked into one of my favorite clothing stores to try on some dresses. I came out of the change room to look at myself in the mirror. (Yes, it was one of those change rooms that doesn't have a mirror inside. I hate that.)

The saleswoman said to me, "Wow, you look great. Didn't you just have a baby?"

I hated to admit it, but I had to. "Um, I had a baby about two years ago," I said.

One of my closest friends had two babies, and after each baby she was back into her pre-pregnancy jeans within a week. Now that's something to be amazed about. It's as close to a miracle as, well, having the darn baby.

But when people tell you that you look great two years after having your child, it loses some of the amazement factor. One, after all, could attend a lot of step classes in two years.

But back to my ass. No matter how many spin classes I do, no matter how many yoga classes I do, no matter how many personal training sessions I endure (during which my trainer makes me do squat after squat), my ass has not returned to its pre-pregnancy shape.

What did this baby do to my ass? Not only does it continue to remain mushy, but it also doesn't have any lift.

Yes, I know a heck of a lot of women who complain about how their boobs changed because they breast-fed and how they hang to their elbows after having kids. But to that I just say buy a better bra. A good bra can lift those babies up to their pre-pregnant glory. But there's not much to do about a saggy, mushy ass. It's not like there's a good bra for your butt.

My trainer just tells me I need to do more squats. I hate squats. Who doesn't? And I'm telling you, no matter how many squats I do, my ass is still flat. One of my friends, who also hates her post-birth ass (her kids are now 5 and 7), says that her nutritionist told her it's all about the carbs. When you eat carbs—like bread and pasta—they go straight to your butt.

But as mothers, we need carbs. We need the energy. Also, it's hard not to eat carbs when all your toddler eats is bread, fries and pasta. My toddler eats only carbohydrates. I always pick at her plate.

There are lots of things I miss now that I have a toddler, like having a life. At the end of a long day with my toddler, I'm so god-damn tired I feel like I got my ass whooped. My saggy, mushy ass, that is.

Old Hag

No good comes out of looking into a mirror with your toddler beside you. You realize your skin is wrinkly, the under-eye bags are permanent, and even though you may still feel 18, being a mother has aged you.

There comes a point in your adult life when you are smacked in the face with an ugly realization: the trendy bar you have frequented for years has been taken over by customers who look barely legal. You think, as you look around, "Where are people my age?"

You can't help but feel old—and out of place. The gal next to you at the bar looks very familiar. Then it hits you. She is familiar. You *do* know her. Oh my god. You used to be her *baby-sitter*.

Then a cute young man comes up to you and says, "Hey! How's it going?" And you feel so good about yourself. A cute guy is talking to you, acting like he's interested, even with all the younger/cuter "barely legals" hanging around and you with a wedding band on your finger. And then the cute young man says, "Don't you remember me? You were my counselor at overnight camp!"

Those moments make you feel old—like you've been there, done that; like the party is over. Is there a senior's special for gin and tonics tonight?

But as awful as the trendy bar experience can be, there's nothing like having a toddler to really make you understand what old is.

Sure, it is kind of fun to realize you can still do a somersault after two decades of not doing somersaults, especially when your toddler thinks it's so cool that you can do one.

That is, it's fun until the next morning, when you wake up and your shoulder is completely fucked up and you realize that you shouldn't be doing somersaults at your age. You wonder if your chiropractor can fit you in for an emergency appointment.

Toddlers make you feel old—physically old. You're out of breath just watching them. I don't understand how my toddler, for example, can spend four or five hours running around in a park and still want to play hide-and-go-seek for another two hours when we get home. All I'm thinking is, "My god, I'm exhausted. I can barely walk on a treadmill for twenty minutes anymore. I want to take a nap. How is it that your legs, half the length of mine, can run twice as fast?"

And toddlers do run fast. One minute they're right beside you, the next they're halfway down the block. They're like superheroes. One minute here, the next way over there. They travel at the speed of light.

But what really gets me is not that toddlers make me feel physically old (who really cares if I can't chase a soccer ball for more than ten minutes?), it's that having a child, I swear, has made me *look* old.

This is really painful.

I can barely stand to look at myself in the mirror anymore—especially in the mornings when I'm brushing my teeth. I look, well, old. And that's unacceptable.

I have a couple of friends in their mid-40s who have never had children. They never wanted any. They look at least ten years younger than their actual age. Which means that they look my age. I swear, this is because they never had children.

They can sleep with both eyes and ears closed. They have time for personal upkeep. They don't have to worry all the time about whether their child is thriving . . . or still alive. They don't have gray hair.

I have always looked younger than my age, partly because I keep my hair long and in a ponytail most of the time. But in the past couple of years, ever since I became a mother, I've noticed that the lines on my forehead and the lines around my eyes are starting to show. I have gray hair!

Sure, you can say, this has to do with actual aging, and this is what happens when you hit your 30s. Nope, I think not. I think it has more to do with having a child. You don't start looking older when you're in your 30s just because you're in your 30s. You start to look old in your 30s because this is when you're having babies, and raising toddlers.

Some mornings—especially the mornings after the nights when my daughter has cried out for me a dozen times—I look at myself in the mirror and think, "I would look better right now if I were a crack addict."

I've gotten over the fact that I now eat dinner at 5 p.m., like a senior citizen, because that's when my daughter eats. I've accepted the fact that I don't like to go to bars anymore because all people do at bars is drink. I don't like waking up feeling hungover. I especially don't like feeling hungover while simultaneously looking like a strung-out junkie.

Never hold your toddler close to you in front of a mirror. Toddlers' skin is just so smooth and so, well, free of wrinkles. Even if you're not super wrinkly, if you are an adult and find yourself looking into a mirror next to a toddler, you will look like a raisin. You will regret all those years you suntanned.

I'm not sure what to do about this—aside from taking down all the mirrors in my house. What makes it even worse is that I have proof that it's not just me. Even strangers think I look old.

The other night I was so proud of the Fiancé and me. We got the In-Laws to baby-sit. We went to an early movie. We went out for dinner *after* the movie, at about 9 o'clock. I was so friggin' proud that we were actually having a civilized dinner at what used to be a civilized time for us to go out for dinner.

We went to a bar/lounge type of restaurant. That turned out to be a big mistake. We had a cheerleader for a waitress (a waitress whom I may have babysat). Her personality was as perky as her breasts and I was jealous of both. As she walked us to our table, she made perky small talk.

"Any exciting Friday night plans?" she asked.

I looked at her strangely and thought, "This *is* my exciting Friday night plan. We saw a movie and now we're out to dinner . . . at 9 p.m.!"

But I simply answered, not so perkily, "No, we're just grabbing a quick bite."

Then this cheerleader-turned-waitress asked, "Any exciting weekend plans?"

I thought, "Should I tell her we have two kids' birthday parties to attend and that I need to buy my toddler new underwear?"

"Not really," I answered.

"Oh," she responded. "Are you past that stage of life?"

Hello?

How the fuck was I supposed to answer that one? Was I past what stage of life? The "having exciting plans" stage?

Because we didn't have our daughter with us, this cheerleader-turned-waitress couldn't know that we were parents, or that parents never really have "exciting plans." We're just grateful to keep our kids busy and vaguely entertained. I was happy that I had to buy my toddler new underwear. It gave me a Saturday afternoon goal to accomplish. So there it was. I knew I looked old. Even the waitress thought I looked old. Apparently, I looked too old to still be in the "exciting weekend plan" stage of my life.

"You look like you're 24!" the Fiancé said when we sat down, after I complained about the waitress who thought I looked like an old hag. The Fiancé is a sweet man who always tries to make me feel good. But he's also a liar. He'll tell me I don't smell even when I haven't showered for days.

"What a bitch!" I said to the Fiancé after the perky waitress skipped off.

"I don't think she meant anything by it," he said. "She was just making small talk."

"Even if we are parents," I moaned, "does it mean we're past the stage of having exciting weekend plans? Even if you are 78 years old, does that mean you can't have exciting weekend plans?"

"Beck," the Fiancé said, "she's, like, 19 years old. She doesn't know any better."

Yes, she was, like, 19 years old. She had clear skin. She had perky breasts. She was wearing a short-short skirt. And she, no doubt, had exciting weekend plans that didn't include buying underwear for a toddler. I hated her.

She's lucky she got a tip. But here's a tip for all you perky, child-free waitresses: Never ask anyone, especially parents, if they're past that stage . . . of anything. Buying underwear for your toddler is an exciting weekend plan.

It is.

Late Arrivals

Your child-free friends are always late when you meet them for drinks or dinner. Even though twenty minutes isn't much in the larger scheme of things, for a mother, twenty minutes means reading a book to your child, taking a shower or eating a meal. You start to hate these people because they just don't get it: twenty minutes for parents is the equivalent of two hours for non-parents.

People annoy me all the time. During the twenty-five minutes or so I'm out in the morning, dropping my daughter off at school, five people will irritate me.

Drivers who don't come to a complete stop at lights annoy me. The Starbucks barista who takes too long to make my latte annoys me. Strangers who don't hold the door open behind them, even though I'm pushing a stroller, *and am right there behind them*, annoy me.

But nothing annoys me more these days than Late Arrivals.

Mothers don't like going out all that much. As evidence I give you my friend Dana, who was invited to a very fabulous party one recent night. She got dressed, didn't like how her dress looked slightly wrinkly, got out of it, ironed it, got back into her dress, put on her makeup, straightened her hair, looked into the mirror and said, "Who am I kidding?" She proceeded to change out of her dress, put her sweat clothes on, and turn on the television. She was just too tired to go out, even for an hour, though she'd already dressed, showered and done her hair and makeup. She told me, "I even looked good and still didn't want to go."

You know that you've definitely become a parent who doesn't

like going out all that much when a work colleague asks to meet you at 7 and you send an e-mail back asking if they mean 7 a.m. or 7 p.m.

Without a doubt, you'll know you're different from your child-free colleague (who still likes to go out after work) when she writes back as if you've asked the stupidest question ever: "Seven p.m., of course! Unless you want to have the meeting in my bed, because that's where I'll be at 7 a.m."

"I'm sorry," you want to e-mail back, "but I have *a toddler*. I *am* awake at 7 a.m. and 7 p.m. Really, it's not such a ridiculous question to ask."

So, when mothers do make plans to go out, it's a big deal. And you shouldn't be late. It's so disrespectful!

I know. Anyone reading this who knew me just a couple of years ago will think I'm the biggest hypocrite in the world. I used to be the one who was always late. And not just five minutes late (which is okay) and not even ten minutes late (still passable). Sometimes I used to be an hour late.

This makes me sound like a very selfish person. And, you know what? I was a completely selfish person to be that late. I'd like to apologize to everyone I was ever late meeting. I'm sorry. I'm so sorry. I'm so sorry. Sorry. Sorry. (I'd have to say this ten million times to make up for it.)

Now, many new mothers *are* late when meeting you, especially if they have to bring their baby along. This is because they just can't get their shit together. And I don't mean this in a bad way. Hey, I've been there. You've gotten your child all dressed in her hat and coat and scarf and managed to wrangle on her mittens, even though she doesn't quite get the concept of the thumb hole. You've accomplished this only to find yourself sniffing something not quite kosher, which means you have to undress your kid, change her diaper and start all over again.

I know that getting a baby or a toddler out of the house to buy a carton of milk across the street can take an hour and a half.

My daughter loves her Saturday morning dance classes. But the dance class is only forty-five minutes long. It takes me three times as long as that to get her ready and out the door. Sometimes, it takes more than two hours for her to wake up, eat, get dressed, brush her teeth and her hair, and put on her dance outfit, which includes a bodysuit, tights and tutu. Which is why I get up at 4 a.m. on Saturday mornings to get to this forty-five-minute dance class at 10:30 a.m. At least that's what it feels like.

I'm always on time nowadays. Not only am I always on time, I'm always a few minutes *early*, which is what happens when you are constantly planning four hours in advance to get your child out the door. It becomes routine, even if you're not taking your toddler along with you.

When I meet friends for lunch or a drink, I start getting ready *three hours* before I need to leave the house. My non-mother friends, however, are still always late. And why wouldn't they be? They don't go through the same thought process as I do before we meet, which goes something like this: Okay, I have to be somewhere at 7 p.m. I have to take a shower and dry my hair and get dressed. The toddler will be running around while I shower and dry my hair and get dressed, wanting to show me her underpants 3,000 times and help me put my bra on. Then she'll want to "help" me "style" my hair, which will put me at least a half-hour behind. Then my toddler will decide that it's a "fantastic idea" to take one of my boots, while I'm putting the other one on, and run around the house. I'll have to chase her. It will take me at least fifteen minutes to convince her that I need my boot and that THIS IS NOT A GAME. Then I won't be able to find my keys, because my toddler thinks it's also a "fantastic idea" to hide things. That will put me back at least another twenty minutes because, of course, she won't remember where exactly she hid my keys. And then there's the actual goodbye, which can set me back anywhere from fifteen to thirty minutes as I try to explain that I'm going out for only a little while, not forever, and that I will be back and that I can't actually leave the house while she's holding onto my leg for dear life, so can she please, please, please let go of me?

This is why I start getting ready at 2 p.m. for a 7 p.m. drink date. I know if I don't get ready for the drink *practically the day before*, I'll end up being late.

Usually, when I meet a friend, I'm sweating by the time I arrive at the destination (after chasing my toddler to get my boot back and using all my upper body strength to tear her off my leg). I'm definitely already exhausted. But if I'm meeting a non-mother friend, I usually find myself sitting alone for at least fifteen to twenty minutes. Non-mothers have nothing to rush for.

I do, though. Mainly, I want to rush home. Because even though my toddler drove me nuts—drove me sometimes to the point of drinking, which is why I'm out in the first place—I still want to be back in time to say goodnight. At the very least I want to get home in time for a solid nine-hour sleep. After all, I have a toddler to deal with the next morning.

Non-mother friends, in my experience, don't understand what a hassle it is to get out the door. And why would they? All they have to do is put on mascara and lip gloss. They have all the time in the world—la de da. If they're twenty minutes late, it's no big deal.

Here's the thing: IT'S A FUCKING BIG DEAL.

In the twenty minutes that my non-mother friends leave me sitting and waiting for them, I could have actually washed all the shampoo out of my hair. I could have actually read my child a book. I could have actually eaten more than a banana for dinner.

And still, they never get why I want to leave an hour and a half after I've arrived. "But I just got here," they'll say. "It's still so early!" And I'll think, "Well, if you actually got here on time, we would have had more time. And it's not early. It's a *school night*."

I find myself actually thinking they're selfish for keeping me waiting, even though only a couple of years ago, I was that person. While inside I may be annoyed, I can't actually get outwardly mad at these friends. Getting mad at a non-parent for being late doesn't get you anywhere. It doesn't make them speed up the next time. And you know they'll just think you're being completely unreasonable, because what's the point of getting mad about only twenty minutes?

You can't win being a mother. You have two types of friends: mother friends and non-mother friends. You can't be mad at your mother friends when they're late because they have kids, and you know how kids hold you up. And you can't be mad at your non-mother friends, because they just don't get it. All you can do is remember to bring along a book.

And order a drink while you wait.

Derailed

The fast track to getting off track is called motherhood. You're slowly realizing that motherhood is more important to you than anything else. You start to think ruling the world doesn't matter all that much anymore. Were you once really that ambitious?

I worry that I've lost my edge. You know, that edge that makes you want to succeed in your career and take over the world.

I remember one of my journalism professors—a woman—telling the class that we couldn't "have both." Meaning we couldn't possibly be a successful journalist and have a family. It was an either/or situation.

At the time, I thought it was the most ridiculous statement I had ever heard.

This professor wasn't married, nor did she have children. Did she consider herself successful? What does success really mean?

I wondered what I was doing at this school, with this professor telling me I could either be a good journalist or have a family. I did believe that woman could have it all. Why couldn't you be successful in your career and have a family?

I still don't agree with her. Ten years later (gulp—has it been that long?) I still believe that women can have both. You can have a successful career and have a family. I'm not sure, though, you can do both really well, or at the same time.

Some days, you will be better as a mother than at your job. Some days, you will be better at your job than at being a mother.

I will admit that I've lost some of my edge. I'm not sure how it happened, but while my daughter was learning to walk, to eat on her own, to talk, I realized that I'd lost my edge. And by edge, I mean that overwhelming ambition—the thing that makes you believe that what you do really matters and that you actually like working ten hours a day.

My work hours have changed since having a baby. I used to get high off stress. I used to work six days a week, sometimes seven. I remember not really minding. I remember working twelve-hour days and thinking that was normal.

Now I do mind working that much.

In the pre-motherhood days, I had a little thing called stamina. I don't have it anymore. Maybe it's because I'm still so sleep deprived.

Mostly, now, when I get home from work, I just want to spend time with my daughter. I feel so guilty that I don't spend enough time with her during the day. I used to work at work, and then bring my computer home to continue working. I don't do that any more. Now I leave my computer at the office, get home by 4:00, and rarely check e-mail after that. I don't work on weekends either. Maybe I am a little less ambitious than I used to be, and maybe it is because I'm a mother and realize that my daughter is more important than my career.

But I'm not saying you can't have both. I'm saying that, like the first step in a twelve-step program, you have to accept that maybe you've lost your edge. And maybe that's okay.

I know lawyers who are mothers, who will get up at 4 a.m., go to the office, go back home to have breakfast with their children, go back to work, get home for dinner with their children, and then go back to the office and work until midnight. And then get up again at 4:00. These women don't seem to have lost their edge.

But they seem *stressed*.

In Canada, we are so fortunate to have a year-long maternity leave. However, I know women who go back to work six weeks after giving birth (and one who did after having twins!) because they don't want to give up the positions they worked so hard to get.

Sometimes I think that it's an age thing, that maybe once you hit 30, you start to realize that what you've been working so hard to achieve is really just shallow. It's like people say (and this is depressing): at the end of your life, who is going to be there for you—your work or your family?

I've learned that it's all about family. Once you become a mother, you want to spend more time with your family. You don't want to be checking e-mail every five minutes. You don't want to answer your cellphone after 4 p.m. (not that you can actually talk on the phone with a toddler screaming at you, "Watch me dance, Mommy! Watch me dance!").

As my daughter changes from a baby to a toddler, I find myself wanting to spend even more time with her. Shortly enough, she'll be in school full-time. She'll want to hang out with her friends and I'll never see her. And maybe that's when I'll get back the urge to change the world.

In the meantime, I simply think that my ambition has walked off into the sunset with my "energy."

I hope they're happy together without me.

Super Spies

Most mothers have a second (or third) career. You find yourself hiding behind bushes—wearing a hat and sunglasses—to make sure your child doesn't die under someone else's watch. Will you be caught in the act?

One morning, years ago, I called my best friend during "outdoor playtime."

Of course, back then—being single, childless and in my early 20s—I had no idea it was "outdoor playtime," or even exactly what "outdoor playtime" meant. I was just getting out of bed.

"What are you doing?" I remember asking my best friend sleepily.

"I'm sitting in my car outside my son's daycare. It's outdoor playtime," she said. "Okay," I said slowly. "Why are you sitting in your car outside the school at outdoor playtime?"

"You're right," she responded. "I should get closer. I should get out of the car and hide behind the trees."

To which I responded, "Okay, what the fuck are you talking about?" (I used to swear far more frequently before I became a mother.)

She explained that some of the little people in her toddler's daycare had been picking on her son. She wanted to check out the bullying in action. She wanted to witness it firsthand to find out who the pint-size culprits were.

"Okay, I'm going into the bushes now," she said. "Do you want to come? Or do you want to talk later?"

She was actually whispering into her cellphone, as if we were still in fifth grade and cheating during a test.

I think I probably responded with something along the lines of, "Oh . . . my . . . god. You're psychotic. You need help! Just call me back when you're done spying."

Back then, I really did think she was psychotic. I really did think she needed help. I may have even been naive enough to suggest that she "might want to get a hobby."

That was before I became a mother—and a super-spy.

I've spied on my toddler during her swim class. I've spied on her while she's at pre-school. And before that, I spied on her while she was in her Time for Twos classes.

These days, I don't think there's anything wrong with spying on your children. I'm not talking about Nanny Cams or anything like that—I don't think I'd ever go that far—but I am willing to sneak a peak. I want to make sure that my child is being taken care of to the best of any teenager's ability—teenagers who for sure would rather be sleeping or talking to their boyfriends or eating French fries. Teenagers in whose care I've left my loved one. Teenagers who are getting paid $8 an hour.

Take my toddler's swim class, for example. The instructors seemed so young! (Then again, maybe I've reached the age where everyone is starting to seem young.) Because my toddler doesn't know how to swim, I was naturally concerned that teenagers in charge would make sure she didn't drown.

Especially since my toddler is a liar.

If you ask her if she can swim, she'll answer, "Yes," even though she most definitely cannot. She likes to say she knows how to swim to get out of wearing life jackets or water wings.

Once, we were at a public pool and the Fiancé was about to take our toddler in the water. The water was too cold for me (and, also, I was way overdue for a bikini wax). I was watching from the other end of the pool when suddenly my toddler—who was not yet wearing a life jacket or any other kind of floating device—jumped off the side of the pool, sort of in the direction of the Fiancé, who was already in.

I watched her go under the water. I watched my Fiancé watch her go under the water. I thought, "What the fuck is he doing?" (Now that I'm a mother, I still swear in my head.)

I raced around to the other side of the pool just as my Fiancé was pulling my daughter up. She was fine.

"Why did you just let her jump off the side of the pool and not catch her?" I screamed at him.

"Well, I asked her if she knew how to swim and she said, 'Yes,'" he told me.

How could the Fiancé not know that she was lying? Toddlers lie all the time! They'll tell you they're not tired, when clearly they are. When you ask them what they did that afternoon, they'll say, "park," even though you were with them the entire afternoon and you know you went to the science center. If you ask them what they ate for dinner, they'll say, "soup," even though they ate pizza.

And if you ask them if they know how to swim, they'll say yes, even though they totally don't.

And so, for obvious reasons, the first time I spied was during one of her swim classes. The pool was on the main floor and there was a viewing box on the second level. I went up there and watched.

I watched while my poor daughter stood alone while the teenage "instructors" helped all the other children put on life jackets. I watched as all the other children got into the pool. I watched all the toddlers play in the water. I watched as my toddler stood by the side of the pool, alone, with no life jacket.

My toddler is quite shy. She doesn't speak up for herself. She's so shy, in fact, that these teenage instructors seemed to forget she was even there.

I was getting mighty pissed. Why weren't they paying attention to my toddler? What was wrong with them? Finally, just as I was going to storm down and yell at them, an instructor just happened to turn around and see my toddler standing alone. She put a life jacket on her and helped her into the pool. All was good.

All was *especially* good when my toddler looked up from the water, saw me watching and waving to her, and screamed out, "Mommy! My Mommy is here!" Which totally caught the attention of the instructors, who looked up to see me, now totally aware that "Mommy" was *there*.

Suddenly, the instructors were all over my daughter.

It's like when you see your boss walking over to your cubicle. You suddenly pretend to be working really hard when all you've really been doing for the entire morning is googling your ex-boyfriend's new girlfriend, trying to figure out if she's good looking or not. You act completely different when the Boss is around. And instructors know that although we didn't technically hire them, parents are still the Boss.

I've also spied at my daughter's pre-school, where spying is so not allowed. There's a sign when you walk into the school door that reads, "Parents must wait here until the bell goes off at 11:38 a.m." In other words: "No spying."

But, you know, rules are made to be broken. Occasionally, I will ignore that sign when picking her up and walk straight to her class at 11:28 a.m., a full ten minutes before I'm allowed.

There's a little nook right outside her class, which allows me to poke my head in while my body remains hidden. My daughter doesn't see me at all, but I can watch how she interacts with the other children. Sometimes I can watch as another 3-year-old smacks her on the side of her head with a wooden block. To which I want to scream (but I hold back, because the first rule of being a spy is not to be seen), "That kid just hit my kid! He should go to the Time-out Chair."

I also think, "Why didn't the teacher see that? Why isn't *she* paying attention to my daughter, who just got bonked in the head by that two-foot-tall bully?"

Spying sessions at my daughter's school don't usually last all that long. Usually another kid senses that someone is watching them and will say something like, "Is my Mommy here, too?" which leads to the teacher seeing me and all the kids screaming out, "Is my Mommy here? Is my Mommy here?"

Despite the mayhem I've created, the teacher suddenly seems to be paying much more attention to my daughter—making sure she's participating, and that no other toddler beats the crap out of her.

Teachers, unlike toddlers, aren't stupid. The teacher knows that when I peek my head into the classroom, I'm spying. I have no excuse. I'm not there to take her to a doctor's appointment. I *am* there spying.

I'm not saying you should spy every day, but a sudden "pop in" spy is just fine. I'd suggest doing it at least once a month. Just to keep them (and by them I really mean teenage camp counselors or teachers who are in charge of more than three kids at a time) on their toes. This is what it means to be a mother. It means, occasionally, being a spy. And maybe going out to buy dark sunglasses and a scarf to add to your mommy wardrobe.

Stroller Legs

Your legs are constantly bruised, making you look like a 6-year-old who fell out of a tree. You can no longer wear short shorts, not because you feel too old, but because you have "Mommy Legs." Why don't they put bumpers on strollers?

It was going to be a big night. It used to be that a party was just another party, but I hadn't gone to a party for weeks upon weeks. Maybe even months.

The shindig was to celebrate the anniversary of a fashion magazine. And there was already drama. One ex-friend I definitely didn't want to see would most likely be there. Probably a couple of ex-boyfriends. Gossip columnists.

And, like I said, it was a fashion party, which meant that I had to attempt to look good. The fact is, because I hadn't been to a big blowout in a while, I was actually looking forward to all the drama—even running into the former friend would add some sort of excitement to my usual routine of getting the toddler ready for bed and joining her at 9 p.m., after watching reruns of *Will and Grace*.

This party didn't start until 9 p.m.!

At around 7 p.m., the friend I was going to the party with, who is also the mother of two toddlers, called me.

"Can we please meet for a drink somewhere before we go? I'm going to fade if I don't get out of the house."

I knew exactly what she meant. I had been excited about this party all day, but at around 5 o'clock I had started to crash. I had actually started to think, "Maybe I will bail on this party. What am I going to miss anyway?"

This is what happens when you become a mother.

Sleep becomes more important than anything else in the world. Not even seeing your favorite actor—Johnny Depp, Brad Pitt—makes you 100 percent certain that you want to leave your house, especially if you know you you there's a chance you could fall asleep early and feel refreshed in the morning.

This is a dangerous road to go down, though. As a mother, if I could choose, I would probably stay in every night. But, really, what kind of life is that, leaving an imprint of your ass on the couch watching reruns of *Everybody Loves Raymond*? Sometimes, you must force yourself out of the house after dark, or you're as fun as a nun in a monastery.

This was one of those times. I knew I would probably have fun—if only I could get out of the house before that "I'm starting to fade" feeling really kicked in. So my friend and I decided to meet at a hotel bar prior to the party.

"What are you wearing?" I asked before getting off the phone. (Since becoming a mother, I have started trying less. What does it matter how good I look? I'm a mother! I've already landed the most important person in my life.) "Can I wear jeans?"

"It's a fashion party," my friend said kindly. "You could probably wear jeans but I imagine it's probably a pretty fashionable crowd."

"Well, what are you wearing?" I asked.

"I have this Dolce & Gabanna dress that I haven't worn yet," she told me. "But it's pretty sexy."

I ransacked my closet and found a LBD (little black dress).

I jumped in the shower, and even felt slightly rejuvenated afterward. Wrapped in a towel, I sat on my bed to put some lotion on my legs. And that's when it happened. That's when I realized I could not be seen in public!

I could not believe what I was looking at. There were dozens of bruises on my legs, in all shapes and sizes! My legs looked like two-week-old bananas—bananas that had fallen off the back of a truck and then been run over by a stampede of horses.

How could I possibly wear a LBD with so many bruises on my legs? And, how the heck did I *get* so many bruises on my legs?

Welcome to the world of Mommy Legs.

Mommy Legs are bruised, thanks mostly, I think, to the stroller I lift up and down the stairs, which bangs into my shins and my outer thighs. But there are also bruises from walking into my toddler's table—the one that reaches up to my shins, the one that I walk into, every time I walk by. There are the bruises from jumping out of bed and walking into my dresser after the alarm goes off. These are definitely mommy bruises.

And Mommy Legs never go away, at least that how it seems. Just as one bruise starts to fade, another one appears.

I have so many boo-boos, as my toddler says, I may never be able to wear a short skirt again.

How was I going to go out in a LBD with Mommy Legs?

I put on knee-high boots.

So, if you see us mothers out in jeans it's not because we don't try. At least that's not the only reason. It's because we're hiding our Mommy Legs.

Have some pity, okay?

Call Waiting

Like a doctor, a parent is always on call. You give out your unlisted phone number and you pick up those dreaded "private" calls, just in case. Every call (might) matter after all.

You cannot cut yourself off from the world when you are a mother. No matter how much you'd love to just shut off your cellphone, you cannot do it. This is because you've written down—numerous times for numerous people—an "emergency contact" for your kid.

And you, my friend, *are* the emergency contact. (That reminds me. I really should not have my ex-boyfriend still listed as the emergency contact on my hospital card. It's been a decade since we broke up and at least eight years since I've spoken to him and if they ever called him from the hospital to come get me, he'd probably be, like, "Rebecca? Rebecca who?")

Since my baby has become a toddler and actually goes places where I can drop her off, I've filled out more forms, and written down my cellphone number more times than I can count. I'm not saying jail would be a good experience, and neither is being in the hospital, but I think both places give you an excuse to cut yourself off from the world. When I was single and working a heck of a lot, I used to love getting on an airplane, simply because I knew that for those short hours, no one could get in touch with me.

Now, it's all about call waiting. And I'm not talking about that annoying beep when someone is trying to get through and you're on your phone. I'm talking about literally waiting for a call.

You are constantly waiting for a call to tell you your kid is sick or has lice and must be taken home immediately.

I feel guilty when I shut off my phone in yoga class. I feel guilty shutting off my phone when I meet with someone for business. I feel guilty for shutting off my phone and trying to take a forty-five-minute nap.

I once missed an "emergency contact" call. I would like to say I was in the middle of doing something really important—like conducting a business conference call or saving children in a third-world country—but I'd actually gone back to bed at 10 a.m. and was sleeping. As I was drifting off, I had the thought that this nap would come back and bite me in the ass. I was right.

I heard my cell ringing downstairs and I just thought, "Oh, whatever. It can wait."

Well, an hour later, the Fiancé came home with our toddler.

"The school called and said she wasn't feeling well and they tried to call you but you didn't pick up, so they called me," he said.

"I was in the middle of working!"

I learned my lesson.

The thing about being a mother and an emergency contact is that you can no longer not pick up a "private call." You can no longer not answer a number when you don't recognize it.

Which sucks because it's always the person you least want to talk to. And yet, that "private number" could be someone calling from your toddler's dance class or daycare or camp. You pick up and end up talking to your cellphone provider about their special deals.

The other thing about being a mother is you can't get sick. You just can't. I mean, you can, and you do, but it's not like being sick was when you were single and childless. Toddlers don't let you lie in bed and cry and feel sorry for yourself.

Your toddler is not going to make you chicken soup. You still have to be a mother.

You're on-call, 24/7. Forever.

Mean Mommy Voice

You will hear this tone of voice coming from your own mouth. You absolutely loathe this tone. You never even knew you had this tone until your toddler told you about it. You wonder, how did I turn into this person?

I didn't come up with this. I swear to god. But, apparently, according to my 2-year-old, I have a Mean Mommy Voice. The first time I heard her tell me I had a Mean Mommy Voice, I was, like, "Oh my god. I have a Mean Mommy Voice?!?"

I know that voice. I've heard other mothers use that voice.

Once, when I was at Pottery Barn one early morning, I was watching a mother with a newborn in a baby carrier. Her toddler was running through the store. He was picking up and touching everything. As well as watching this mother, I was listening.

"Don't touch that," this mother said. "Stay still."

"Don't touch that!"

"Stay still!"

"Put that down!"

"Don't touch that!"

I thought, at the time, that this poor mother was probably just exhausted, with a newborn and a terror of a toddler. But I also thought she had a Mean Mommy Voice. This woman's voice did sound mean, like that teacher you always remember (and not in a good way). As I pushed my baby through the store in her stroller, I also thought, "God, I hope I don't sound like that one day."

Little did I know that we all have Mean Mommy Voices just waiting to come out.

My daughter had gotten out of bed for the umpteenth time

that night. And it had already been a long day. The thing is, I've never been a yeller. If you make me mad, I won't yell at you. I'll ignore you.

"Get back to bed now," I said sternly and loudly (but not yelling). At which she started to cry. Which isn't unusual. She usually starts to cry. But then she said, "Mommy, don't use your mean voice."

I was shocked. Not because my daughter actually knew the word "mean," but because she thought I had a mean voice. (When did she learn the word "mean," anyway?)

I felt horrible! I didn't want to have a Mean Mommy Voice. It just came out that way.

I apologized.

I know. I apologized to my 2-year-old. But, like I said, I didn't want to have a Mean Mommy Voice and I didn't want my daughter to hear my Mean Mommy Voice. I didn't want to be like that woman at Pottery Barn.

"I'm sorry," I told her. "I promise not to use my Mean Mommy Voice. But can you please go back to bed?"

"Okay, but don't use your Mean Mommy Voice," she sobbed.

It's amazing how toddlers know what words will just knife you in the heart. I apologized again. Sometimes I think I'm not so good at this mothering thing. Should I really be apologizing to a little girl who should have been in bed three hours ago? But I so do not want my daughter to think of me as Mean Mommy.

A few days later, she said it again, after I told her not to throw her apple juice box on the floor. "Don't use your Mean Mommy Voice," she said to me after I said, "That's not what we do with empty apple juice boxes!"

"Okay," I told her. "I won't use my Mean Mommy Voice. But throw your juice box in the garbage."

In the bath later that evening my daughter thought it would

be "fantastic," as she said, to take the shampoo and pour it over the ledge and onto the floor.

"Shampoo is for hair," I told her sternly. "It is not for drawing pictures on the floor."

"Mommy, don't use your Mean Mommy Voice," she said pathetically.

"Okay, I won't. But please put down the shampoo," I said.

Even later, when she got out of bed for the eighteenth time, I yelled, "Go to bed!" (Okay, who am I kidding? Sometimes I do yell.)

She started to cry. "Mommy, I don't want you to use your Mean Mommy Voice."

I realized that in a few short hours I had used my Mean Mommy Voice *three* times.

One of my best mother friends told me that her 3-year-old tells her not to wag her finger.

"I never knew I was a finger-wagger," she moaned, "until my daughter kept saying, 'Don't wag your finger at me. Stop wagging your finger at me!'"

My friend thought it was horrible that she was a finger-wagger, just like I think it's horrible that I have a Mean Mommy Voice.

Still, I think I'd much rather be a finger-wagger. At least I wouldn't sound mean.

Trips Are for Kids

There is a world of a difference between going away with your toddler and going on a vacation. If you go away with your toddler, it is not a vacation. It's a trip.

There's a big difference between a trip and a vacation. I no longer say, "I'm going on vacation." I have a toddler now, and a vacation it is definitely not.

Sure, there may be traveler's insurance, an airplane ride, a sunny destination and a beach at the end, but it's definitely not a vacation.

It's a trip.

You learn the difference once you start traveling with a toddler.

Vacations are fun and relaxing. A vacation includes being able to read a few books without any interruptions except from the cabana boy who asks if you'd like a cold towel.

You know you are on vacation when you think to yourself, "Should I just lie here on the beach or go to my hotel room and take a nap?"

You know you're on vacation when you buy yourself a blue-jeweled stone necklace that you know you'll never wear.

You take photos of the sunset on vacation. You drink a lot of wine and sleep in on vacation. There's a lot of wild sex. You may not want to come home when you're on vacation. Ever.

Trips, on the other hand, are what you take once you have children. Trips are piling into a car, or taking two entire days to pack for a three-day long weekend, or getting up twelve hours ahead of time to get to the airport so you won't miss your flight.

Trips usually involve water slides, and waking up at 5:30 a.m., and eating at "child-friendly" restaurants and reapplying sunblock every five minutes. You know you are on a trip because you end up asking yourself, "Why did I ever think this would be a good idea?"

On trips, the only thing you're buying is a Mickey Mouse doll, even though you've tried to explain, unsuccessfully, that you can get that doll anywhere, and that something a little more reminiscent of Spain might be better.

Trips are when you yell at your child, "Smile! Smile goddammit for the camera, so we have some memories of this!"

On trips, you end up sleeping with your child while your partner sleeps on the couch. There is no sex.

On trips you want to come home. It's the only way you can get your toddler back into pre-school.

I read all the time about "child-friendly" hotels, which are a nice thought. But even the most child-friendly resort is not a boarding school. They don't take your kids all day long. They don't put them into bed. They don't bathe them. They don't have to cover the airplane seat with a magazine when they're deboarding because your toddler had an "accident."

A vacation you look forward to planning. With a trip you find yourself screaming at your travel agent, "How can it be $13,000 for one week? It's usually one-quarter of that price," and end up being told, "It's Christmas vacation."

Trips are built around the school "schedule."

Vacations are something you'll miss.

How will you know for sure if you've been on a trip? Easy. You'll feel like you need a vacation after you come home.

Part II
Relationships Turned Relationshits

Jack: Mommy, where is Stephen?
Mommy: Who, Jack?
Jack: You know, Mommy. That man who you are married to.

Jack, 4½, son of Corina Busby

Sleeping Rearrangements

You start off the night with your partner, in a bed. In the morning, he wakes up on the pullout couch in the spare room, you wake up on the hallway floor and your toddler is sleeping soundly in the king-sized bed with the 800-thread-count sheets and the good pillows. It's so a night (not) to remember.

This morning I woke up in my daughter's princess bed.

My daughter was not beside me. She was sleeping soundly in the marital bed—alone. She looked pretty damn comfortable when I went to check on her after detangling myself from her Disney sheets.

Of course she looked comfortable. How could she not be? She had an entire king-size bed to herself, complete with the 800-thread-count sheets and the good pillows that make you feel like you're sleeping on a cloud. We ordered the pillows from a hotel, for exactly that reason. They seriously make you feel like you're sleeping on a cloud.

The Fiancé was in the spare bedroom, moaning about his back and swearing not so quietly.

The spare bedroom has one of those pullout couches that turns into a bed when you pump it up with air. The pump that blows air into this spare bed looks exactly like the kind of pump clowns use to make balloon animals. For god's sake, how comfortable can a bed really be if you have to blow it up with the same kind of pump clowns use to make balloon animals? Sleeping in a bathtub is probably more comfortable than sleeping on our pump-up bed in the spare bedroom. So I understood why the Fiancé was all, "Fuck! My back! Fuck! I didn't sleep at all! Fuck! I can't believe I have to go to work like this."

My daughter's princess bed is a tad more comfortable than the pullout, pump-up bed—aside from her sheets, which are about as comfortable as sleeping on sandpaper. Someone should really come up with 500-thread-count Dora the Explorer and Disney sheets, because parents end up sleeping in children's beds as often, if not more often, than their actual damn children do.

I know that when I went to bed last night, I was with the Fiancé in the marital bed, and our daughter was in her bed. I am never quite sure how I end up where I do each morning. For the last two years, ever since our daughter moved into her Big Girl's Bed, I wake up feeling like I just spent the previous night getting drunk after mixing too many red wines and vodka tonics. Remember when you *used* to ask yourself, after mixing red wine and vodka tonics all night, "How exactly did I get home?" Well now, being a mother, the question is, "How did I end up in this room?"

Like a bad hangover, the events of the previous night start foggily coming back to you. *Oh, right. That's what went down.*

I think the Fiancé and I were sleeping soundly when our daughter came into our room, crying and wanting to sleep with me. It was sometime after 1 a.m.

The Fiancé has one main rule, which is that our toddler can't sleep in our bed. Ever.

Which means, usually, that I end up going back to bed in our daughter's room. But, last night, thinking the Fiancé was sound asleep—and mostly because I was too fucking tired to get out of bed to take my toddler back into her bedroom—I just pulled her up beside me. I tried to remain as close to the edge of the bed as possible with her, without falling off, so the Fiancé would not know she was there.

Which is ridiculous.

Of course he *knew* she was in bed with us. She was screaming, "I want to sleep in your bed," while I was harshly saying, "Shhh!!!! Be quiet! Daddy won't let you sleep here! So you have to be quiet."

But even if she hadn't been crying and screaming, "I want to sleep in your bed," the Fiancé would have woken up.

Toddlers sleep in the most ridiculous positions.

Our daughter likes to sleep horizontally and sometimes diagonally. I remember, at one point, literally pulling her with me to the other end of the bed (so our feet were next to the Fiancé's head) to give him more breathing room. This also seemed like a position that would prevent our toddler's arms from smacking his face.

The next thing I remember is the Fiancé swatting my foot away from his face—I think, rather *I know*, I had kicked him—and him stomping out of the room, huffing, "Thanks for kicking me in the face!"

I remember thinking, "I wonder if he's just going to the washroom."

And then I remember wondering, "I wonder if he is ever going to return—not just to our bed, but to our home. Ever."

Well, three hours later, I knew the answer. The Fiancé hadn't returned to our bed. I know this only because my daughter woke me up at 4 a.m. by lying on top of me. The rest of the bed was empty.

That was the point at which I realized that I couldn't sleep in the same bed with her either—what with her suffocating me—so I went to sleep in her room. Which is how our family of three ended up in three different bedrooms.

This is, apparently, a common occurrence. One of my friends and her husband always end up in their two sons' twin beds, while their two sons end up in their queen-size. As she puts it, "At a certain point in the middle of the night, it doesn't matter what mattress you end up on. You just want to sleep. You're lucky if you even get a mattress."

It's true. Parent-child sleeping rearrangements can remind you of a three-ringed circus. There's so much happening under one roof, and all in such a short period of time!

I'd estimate that, since my daughter turned 2, I've spent a total of two hours each night in the same bed as my Fiancé. There have been weeks, even months, when I don't sleep in the same bed with him at all. I do this because I know my daughter will just start screaming in the middle of the night for me to sleep with her. Instead of waking up at some ungodly hour to go to her room, I figure it's just easier to start off sleeping in her bed. This way I won't have to drag my body out of bed at 3 a.m. trying not to walk into a wall on my way to get her.

The Fiancé and I will brush our teeth in our washroom and I'll say, "Okay, see you in the morning." And he'll say, "Hope you have a good sleep," and we'll leave each other like we are roommates. It's sad really.

The truth is, when you have children, you will never be sure who you'll wake up with, or where. The only thing you *can* be sure of is that you won't wake up where you first fell asleep, and that you'll be exhausted.

Last week, after a fitful night, I woke up in the hallway on a pile of towels. Somehow, in the middle of the night, I had convinced myself that this was the only place I'd finally get some sleep. The Fiancé was in our daughter's room, my daughter (of course) was in the marital bed, and there was no fucking way I was sleeping in that pump-up thing that's *supposedly* a bed.

There's nothing sadder than waking up on the floor in the hallway . . . alone . . . on a pile of dirty laundry. Trust me.

And it gets worse, or so I hear, when you have more than one child.

"It was like a revolving door last night," my friend moaned to me about the Sleeping Rearrangements with her husband, her toddler, Ava, and Wyatt, her 7-month-old son. She sounded like she had been run over by a truck.

The night started out hopefully enough, she explained. She and her husband went to bed at 11, but at 1 a.m., Wyatt started to cry. Her husband went in to calm him. Ava awoke, thanks to her brother's wails, so my friend went into Ava's room to deal with her. But Wyatt wouldn't stop crying, so she went to help her husband. Then Ava started calling out for "Daddy."

Daddy went to Ava, while Mommy went back to her own bedroom with Wyatt.

Then Ava wanted Mommy, so Mommy put Wyatt back into his crib, calmed him, and then went to Ava's room, while Daddy went back to their marital bed. Then Wyatt started crying again.

"I ended up on the couch with the baby. And that all happened between 1 a.m. and 4 a.m.," my friend said, before adding, "Can you tell me what day of the week it is?"

There's definitely one thing you *never* want to ask your partner after a night of Sleeping Rearrangements—especially if he ends up on the spare pump-up bed after being kicked in the face by your un-manicured foot, with toenails so sharp you could probably scale up a tree.

That question is, "So how did you sleep last night?"

Because the response is always, "Fuck! My back! FUCK!"

Date Night

Though you never ever thought in a million years you would be the type of person to utter the phrase "date night," you find yourself looking forward to them. This has nothing to do with keeping the romance alive in your relationship, and everything to do with not having to put your toddler to bed.

"Date Night" takes on a whole new meaning once you become a parent. No longer do you worry about shaving your legs. No longer do you put on your lucky underwear, *just in case*. No longer do you remember to put on deodorant and pretty scented lotions, as you did when you were single, childless and dating.

After you have a baby with your partner/husband and you are what people describe as "settled," Date Night brings a whole different kind of "excitement." When you're "settled" and going out on Date Night, you don't wonder if this could be "it," if he could be the One—or if he's going to kiss you at the end of the night.

You don't worry that you're a slut because you want to sleep with him after the first or second date, or even before you actually go out on the date. (It happens.) But you do get excited. Oh yes. Parents get excited about going out for Date Night because, if we plan our Date Nights right, we'll arrive home *after* the child is asleep.

This, hands down, is the most important aspect of a post-child Date Night. It doesn't matter who pays, if the dinner was good, if you have witty banter with your partner, if he holds the car door open for you or if you "connect."

All that matters is that you arrive home *after* the toddler has fallen asleep. That's the new romance. That's a successful Date Night.

Before I had a child, I never understood why my best friend, now the mother of four, had weekly Thursday night dates with her husband. Now I get it.

Date Night for the Fiancé and me usually includes dinner and a movie. We are generally home by 10. I know it sounds sad, but it's not really.

Our child—fingers crossed—should be well asleep by 10. So, all in all, these Date Nights are usually pretty successful.

Actually, we've had some good Date Nights—early dinner, early movie, sighs of relief when we walk in and hear the words every parent of a toddler wants to hear from the baby-sitter—which are not, "She was really good. Everything was fine," but, "She fell asleep about an hour ago."

But, like bad blind dates—where you're scheming, over appe-tizers, about how you can fake sudden food poisoning because the guy sitting across from you a) is so painfully boring, or b) has just asked if you use a vibrator and if you like having your toes sucked—Date Nights for parents can also turn out horribly.

Like last night. The In-Laws offered to sit. I actually got out of my sweat pants and into jeans, which means I was trying to look good and not like I was just heading to the gym, which is how I mostly look these days (even if I haven't been to the gym in weeks). Mostly I gave up trying to look good at the same time I became a parent.

It just kind of happens, like planned Date Nights just kind of happen.

The Fiancé and I had planned on eating an early dinner at 6 p.m. and then seeing a movie next door to the restaurant at 7:15 p.m. It wasn't even a movie I had heard of. But when you have the chance for a Date Night—even if you don't want to see any movies out there—you pick a damn movie. It's better than getting drunk and it's better than putting your child to bed. You may leave a bad movie disappointed, but at least there's no hangover in the morning and at least you didn't have to wrestle your kid into her pajamas again.

We raced to the restaurant, which luckily had room in their bar area. We sat down and ordered appetizers and our main meal. Unfortunately, the service was very slow, which usually doesn't bother me all that much, except when I have to catch a 7:15 movie.

Our meals arrived at 7:08 p.m., which meant we were paying the bill as we were still eating. I left the restaurant still eating the crusts of my fancy pizza. I was fine with that, though. As a parent I mostly eat standing up. I rarely have sit-down meals, what with a toddler who wants a spoon, then a fork, then more apple juice, then her Barbie bowl. In fact, I can eat an entire meal in three-and-a-half minutes now. I've timed it.

We walked over to the movie theater only to see a sign on the door. There was a "special event" that night and no movies would be playing.

"I can't believe this!" the Fiancé moaned. "This is just our luck."

"I kind of feel sick from eating so fast," I moaned.

"Now what?" he asked. "We can't see a movie. What do you want to do?"

It was a good question. *Now what?*

We had already eaten dinner. It was only 7:15 p.m. There was no way in hell I was going to go home. *The toddler would still be up.*

Though I *was* exhausted, and what I really wanted to do was curl up in a ball on the couch and watch television. But at home was the toddler. And this was Date Night!

"Yes, now what?" I asked.

It was raining so we couldn't just kill time by walking around. And that's what Date Night really turns out to be when you are a parent. It's all about killing time—so you don't have to go home and put your child to sleep.

One of our couple friends will literally drive around and around on their Date Nights (they call them "nights off," because they don't like the term Date Night) to make sure they don't get back home until their child is asleep.

But I get carsick quite easily and don't like being in cars longer than I have to.

"I wish I were a dessert person," I told the Fiancé. "That way we could at least go out for dessert."

We decided to drive to another movie theater in the faint hope that we hadn't missed the movie. Of course, you realize that all early movies (movies for parents) start at around 7 p.m. and the late shows don't start until 9:55 p.m.

Pre-parenthood, I would always go to late movies. But now 9:55 p.m. seems like an impossibly late start time for a movie. We wouldn't be home until midnight and that was ridiculous. Who the hell can stay up until midnight? Who wants to?

"We could go to the magazine store," the Fiancé said.

"Great. That should kill an extra ten minutes," I said.

And so we did. And another ten minutes was killed.

"So what now?" he asked, after we'd purchased magazines we didn't need or want.

"Fuck it. Let's just go home," I said. This Date Night was a bust and the only thing more pathetic than a bust of a date night, is the, "So now what?" conversation.

The Fiancé drove slowly. Seriously, people with canes were walking faster than we were driving. We arrived back at home at 8:05 p.m.

There was a chance that our toddler would be in bed. She is *supposed* to be in bed at 7:15 p.m.

There was a chance—although it was only a one percent chance. This was because her grandparents were baby-sitting and they like to spend time with her, which means they'll keep her up until whenever because they're "spending time with her." (They also don't have to wake her to go to school and see what she's like when she doesn't get enough sleep.)

My heart sank as I walked through the back door and into the kitchen to see my daughter not only not asleep, but not even in bed—and not only not asleep and not in bed, but not even changed into her pajamas.

I felt like the biggest loser in the entire history of daters.

Sure, when you're single and childless, you may have bad dates. But when you actually have a child and a loving fiancé and you have a bad Date Night and you're home at 8:05 p.m., it really is much more depressing. You don't even get a good story to tell your girlfriends the next morning. It's too embarrassing.

"You guys are home so early!" the In-Laws exclaimed.

Even the In-Laws thought we were pathetic for coming home so early, even though we explained what happened. You know when two 70-somethings think you are home "so early," you really, really are pathetic.

It was back to being a mother. I changed my toddler, brushed her teeth, put her into bed, and raced up and down the stairs twelve times during the following hour.

One of my mother friends, who has done the Date Night thing with her husband for years, says, "You have to do it. But when I ask him if we're still on for Date Night, he's like, 'You still want to?' We're both always so tired. We force ourselves to do it."

The only without-fail good thing about post-child Date Nights is that you don't have to worry if your "date" is spending the night or how to get them to leave the next morning without being rude. You don't have to worry if you'll ever hear from them again.

And, in a way, even having a bust of a Date Night is still somehow better than all that.

Not in Front of the C-H-I-L-D

Your voice is raised. Your partner's voice is raised. You're in mid-fight. And your toddler tells you to "Stop that!" You feel like the worst parent in the world and think about sending yourself to the naughty chair (even though your partner was totally wrong and should apologize).

Shocking news! Couples fight!

When you're in a long-term relationship, your partner has the ability to annoy you sometimes, even when they aren't doing anything at all. Seriously. They could just be sitting there reading the paper, minding their own business, but the sound of the paper rumbling annoys you. *Why is he rumbling the paper like that? He's doing it on purpose!*

After you have a baby you'll probably fight more than ever.

This is because, for example, your partner wants to spend five hours golfing on a Sunday afternoon with "the boys," which means you'll be stuck at home taking care of the newborn.

Technically, because you love your partner, you want him to have fun. But you also really don't want him to have fun, especially when you know you're not going to be having fun, too. It's not logical, but that's how you feel (kind of like when your partner is annoying you and you want to be alone, but as soon as he leaves the room, you want him back).

Or maybe you're fighting because your partner works late (and seemingly even later since you had the newborn, or since your toddler has become a living nightmare). It just seems that, suddenly, your partner tells you he has Big Deals that need to be taken care of and he won't be home until after bedtime.

Sleep deprivation will also play a large part in the fighting. When you're sleep deprived, you can barely talk, or remember what day of the week it is. Things that never used to irritate you about your partner suddenly seem like very big annoyances (like that they even dared asked you if they could go golfing. Or that they asked you, "How are you?" *What were they thinking?*).

So you bicker. And bicker, trust me, you will. Often. You'll bicker so much you won't remember any other form of communication.

One of my friends bickered so much with her husband after having a baby that the only way they could communicate without yelling at one another was by e-mail on their Blackberries, even when they were both at home.

Anyway, it's actually fine to fight (or bicker), when you have a newborn. Most of the time, newborns sleep. There are plenty of hours in the day in which to raise your voice while your baby sleeps. Babies don't understand yelling. And, also, it's like they are deaf. They don't seem to hear anything. For example, when my toddler was a newborn, she literally slept through the loudest fire alarm I've ever heard. It lasted close to an hour.

So, a little yelling match between Mom and Dad won't wake Baby. Personally, I believe those couples in serious relationships who never fight are the ones with the real problem. It's not healthy. It's weird. (If you don't fight, how can you have makeup sex, which is the only good thing that comes from fighting in long-term relationships? If you don't fight, when will you get that oh-so-deserved apology . . . and maybe flowers?)

When you become a parent, you will start hanging around with at least a few other couples who also have children. (And, yes, just because you have babies around the same age, you'll convince yourself it's all you need to get along.) Some of these couples look and act so sickeningly sweet to one another it will make you wonder why your own relationship isn't all sugary sweet.

But, trust me, even the parents with the newborn *and* toddler who act like they're still on their honeymoon fight when they're alone.

I know this to be true. Recently, I was at a dinner party. And by dinner party, I mean a bunch of couples with kids running all over the place. "Dinner party" takes on a whole new meaning once you have children. You may have a glass in your hand but the night is full of whine, not wine. Anyway, there was one woman there who was super-sweet, as was her husband. They made me want to vomit. Seriously.

They were just so kind to each other. I'm talking rubbing each other's backs, asking each other if they could get one another something from the kitchen. It was so unnatural. It was gross.

They were so nice to each other that I actually asked this woman, when her husband was out of the room, "Do you two ever fight?"

I couldn't restrain myself. There was definitely something wrong with them. You just wanted to touch them to see if they were human.

"Are you crazy? We mostly fight. We fight more than we don't fight," she answered.

So, it seems, even the sweetest-looking couples do fight when they're alone. Which doesn't bode well for couples who fight publicly. But that's not the point. The point is this: There will come a time when your child starts to understand what's going on around her. She will actually start hearing you. At pre-school children get sent to the "naughty chair" when they fight with each other. And they're told, over and over again, "You two are friends. Say you're sorry to each other and be friends again."

And then, because they are 2- or 3-year-olds, they are friends again. Just like that. And all is forgotten.

Toddlers are told, probably 180 times a day while they are at pre-school or daycare, that fighting is bad, bad, bad. Of course, they're only toddlers and don't get the intricacies of adult relationships. Grown-up relationships are complicated. It's not like when toddlers get mad at each other because, "Ella is using the pink play dough and I wanted the pink play dough."

Toddlers don't get that sometimes you just have to fight.

You can't exactly say to your 3-year-old, "No, it's okay to fight when it's Mommy and Daddy who are fighting, because Daddy is being an ass."

The Fiancé and I were arguing about something recently. I can't even remember how it started. That's the thing with sleep-deprived fights—you're so tired you can't even remember why you're fighting in the first place. You just know you're pissed at each other.

In any case, our voices were raised. Suddenly, our toddler said, "You two have to be nice to each other. Stop fighting."

Hello, guilt trip!

I've never felt so guilty in my life. I could tell the Fiancé felt bad, too. He and I just looked at each other lovingly and said, "I love you. I'm sorry." Then we kissed each other and made up.

Okay, that's so not what happened. We continued to give each other dirty looks. But we did stop fighting. We had to. Because when your own toddler tells you to be "nice to each other" you feel bad. You actually feel like you should be sending yourself to the naughty chair. It's bad to fight in front of your child. Bad, bad, bad. Mostly because it makes your child feel bad.

So, at present, or at least during the last couple of weeks, there have been no major blowouts between the Fiancé and me. We have not raised our voices at one another. At least not in front of our toddler.

When I told my friend about the episode, she tried to make me feel better. She and her husband argue all the time, she told me, in front of their children.

"I read about an expert who said it was actually good to fight in front of your kids, as long as your kids see you resolve the problem," she told me. "Then they can learn from that." (Sure, keep telling yourself that.)

That would be great, if I believed it. Or if I could remember what the heck the Fiancé and I were fighting about in the first place. If you can't remember what you're fighting about in the first place, you have no idea what issues you have to resolve.

So, remember: unless you're prepared to sit in the naughty chair, don't argue. At least not in front of the C-H-I-L-D.

Good Cop/Bad Cop

This is the position you find yourself in, or choose for yourself, once you realize your toddler is completely out of control, and that it may not be such a bad idea for one of the grown-ups in the household to start disciplining. Which one are you?

I am good at a few things. I can type really fast. I can predict who the next American Idol will be at the start of the season. I can make the perfect hard-boiled egg. But I am not good at being the Bad Cop.

When you have a baby with someone, and that baby turns into a toddler, and that toddler starts doing bad things—like refusing to go to bed, or grabbing toys from another kid's hands, or dropping your cellphone in the toilet—someone in the household has to be the Bad Cop. Someone has to be the mean one and tell the child to stop doing bad things. There are only so many cellphones a person can go through before the salesperson at the cellphone store says, "Gee, you look really familiar. Weren't you just in here last week?"

I should mention, also, that I'm bad at a lot of other things, as well. I'm bad at remembering to not leave my wet towels on the bed. I'm bad at cooking (except for the aforementioned hard-boiled eggs and no one wants five hard-boiled eggs for dinner). But, most of all, I'm bad at disciplining.

By default, then, most of my daughter's disciplining is left up to her father, which automatically makes him the Bad Cop and me the Good Cop. This may not be fair, and for that I'm sorry. But I just cannot seem to be the Bad Cop. I also don't want to be the Bad Cop. I want to be the Good Cop. I want my toddler to *like me*.

The Fiancé and I made a pact after we had our child. I think we even shook on it. That pact was that whatever I told our daughter to do, he would back me up.

So, when I say, "It's time for bed," he's supposed to repeat, "It's time for bed."

The other part of the pact was that whatever the Fiancé told our child to do, I would back him up. So when he says, "You do not play with carving knives," I, too, am supposed to say, "You do not play with carving knives."

The Fiancé has kept up his end of the pact. When I say, "You cannot have any more candy before you go to bed," he'll take the box away from our toddler and back me up by repeating, "You can't have any more candy."

I, however, have not kept up my end. Except when it comes to things like playing with carving knives. I agree, she can't play with knives. But when it comes to things like, um, bedtime, I'm a complete sucker. My daughter is just too cute for me to be the Bad Cop. She looks at me with her big brown eyes and I melt, even though I am usually super-frustrated and can't wait for her to fall asleep.

I *want* her to go to bed. I just don't *want* to yell at her. I *want* her to stop putting stickers on the fridge. I just don't *want* to yell at her.

I've come to think that when people get married, it wouldn't be such a bad idea to include a Good Cop/Bad Cop clause in the prenuptial agreement. That way, everyone's clear ahead of time about the role they are going to play. And there will be no arguments that start with, "I'm always the one yelling at her! It's your turn!"

I watch my other friends with children to see how this issue is handled in their homes. It's very rare that I witness both parents being the Bad Cop. Sometimes it's the mother who is the Bad Cop, reprimanding her children while Dad sits back drinking a beer and watching "the game," oblivious to his toddler, who has smeared chocolate pudding on the carpet. Sometimes it's the father who's on Bad Copy duty, chasing after the kids while Mom sits back sipping a glass of wine and talking about her new laser hair treatments, oblivious to her toddler, who has smeared chocolate pudding on the carpet. I can tell who's the Bad Cop and who's the Good Cop simply by the way they react after their child thought it was a good idea to throw all their toys into the fireplace.

So, back to the bedtime thing. Yes, when the Fiancé says to our toddler, "It's time to go to bed," I'll say, "Yup, it's time to go to bed," and I'll take our daughter upstairs to her bedroom.

But then something happens, and the next thing you know we're having pillow fights or I'm hiding under the covers with her with a flashlight. What definitely is not happening is bedtime. Why not?

Exactly.

I just cannot be the Bad Cop who yells, "It's time to go to bed!!!!"

I like to think of myself as the kind of laid-back mother who's all, like "La de da, things will all work out, and so what if she doesn't go to bed, or wants to put her French fries in her cup of milk? So be it. If she wants to wear eighteen Band-Aids on her knee, so be it. She's a toddler! And that's what toddlers are supposed to do, aren't they?"

Being the Good Cop also works out for me because I am a really good actor. Let's say our daughter gets out of bed for the umpteenth time. I'll just moan to the Fiancé, "You go up and yell at her. She listens to you better. I've tried so hard. It's your turn." I'll say this even though I really haven't tried all that hard. Or barely at all.

But it is sort of true.

Because the Fiancé has become the Bad Cop our daughter *does* listen to him more than she listens to me, which doesn't bode well for the future. Like when she'll tell me she wants to go away for the weekend with a boy I've never met whose name is Cougar. I know all this. But still.

One of my mother friends says she's always been the Bad Cop. "I'll always be yelling, 'No!' to my kids and my husband will say, 'Why are you always saying no? Why don't you think about what you're saying no to before you say it?'"

Her husband is definitely the Good Cop, because usually my friend is saying things like, "No! You cannot put an elastic band around the dog's nose!" while her husband is, like, "I'm sure he'll get bored of this in a minute, honey. Let him be."

Another friend and her husband definitely have not worked out the whole Good Cop/Bad Cop position in their relationship, even after having three kids. When she tells her children that they can't watch *The Simpsons* (should 5-year-olds really be watching *The Simpsons* anyway? Okay . . . no judgment) and they must go to bed, her kids will now say, "But Daddy said we could watch it." To which she says to her husband, "Fine! They can watch. But *you're* putting them to bed then." Either way, she comes across as the Bad Cop—in her marriage and as a mother.

Though I freely admit I want to be the Good Cop (and am the Good Cop), this works only because the Fiancé doesn't mind the role of the Bad Cop. He lets me play my Good Cop role and I let him play his Bad Cop Role. We're lucky that way. And the people around us are lucky, too.

There is nothing worse than watching your friends argue in front of you about disciplining their toddler. One recent morning at a coffee shop, I watched as two of my married friends almost got into a full-on blowout after my friend ripped her toddler's donut in half. Their kid was screaming, "I don't want the donut in half. I want it whole. I don't like it when it's in half. I want it whole!"

My friend, definitely the Good Cop, was about to get up and

buy him another donut, but her husband—the Bad Cop—was all, like, "No, he has to learn that he can't get everything he wants. You are not getting him a new donut."

Their toddler kept screaming . . . and screaming . . . and screaming.

On the one hand I was, like, "Okay, your husband is right. He does have to learn that he can't get everything he wants and that a donut tastes the same if it's whole or ripped in half."

But the Good Cop in me was, like, "Get the kid another fucking donut and let this nightmare end."

My friend did end up getting her toddler another donut, while her husband sighed and shook his head with a pissed-off look on his face. I'm sure they went home and fought about it. Which is why it's not such a bad idea to have a disciplining paragraph in a pre-nup.

I know one day I am going to have to be the Bad Cop. It's inevitable. But for now, I'm sticking to, "She just listens to you better, honey."

I like being *liked*. I know, in time, my toddler will hate me.

Plus, I never *signed* anything.

Tit for Toddler

If you go to a yoga class and leave your partner with the child for two hours, it will come back to bite you in the ass. He'll expect to get two hours off to go out with his friends. On and on it goes.

I've never witnessed as much "tit for tat" as I have since becoming a mother.

I don't like the tit for tat.

It's like back when you were dating and your new-ish boyfriend goes for coffee with his ex-girlfriend, so you call your ex-boyfriend and make plans to see a movie. "Well, you went for coffee so why shouldn't I go for a movie with my ex?" you'll say.

No good comes out from the tit for tat. And, yet, I watch parents do it all the time.

"I'm not going to that birthday party," one of our male friends said when I asked if he was attending the birthday bash of a mutual friend's toddler. "My wife's going away for a week for work, so that means I don't have to go. She has to."

Or the Fiancé will get calls from his male friends to go out for drinks. They'll say their wives went out the night before so now it's their turn to party.

Maybe the tit for tat is inevitable once you become parents, as opposed to just lovers. But it's just so unromantic. Then again, asking your partner to go buy you tampons on his way home from work or letting him see your stretch marks isn't that romantic either.

However, like stretch marks, the tit for tat never goes away. Once you go down that road—"Well, you went to a movie and I had to watch Timmy, so now I get to go to a concert while you baby-sit"—it never ends.

"You went to a concert," leads into "So I deserve a facial," which leads into, "Well you got a facial, so I'm going away for the weekend with the boys to see the game," which leads into, "Well, you went away with the boys for the weekend to see the game, so I get to go away to a spa for a week," which leads into, "Well, you went away to a spa for a week, so I'm going to buy a new car," which leads into, "Well, you bought a new car, so I want a new house," which may lead into, "Let's just get a divorce."

The point is, once you start down that road, it's the longest road in the world. You may as well shell out for a baby-sitter so you can both go out. It's a hell of a lot cheaper than couple's counseling.

I Keep Falling in Love

It's a different kind of love, but your heart pitter-patters when you watch the father of your toddler hang out with your toddler. You've never been so turned on in your life (though you are way too tired to do anything about it).

I fell in love with my fiancé all over again after we had a child.

Sure, there are still moments when I want to wring his neck. And to be fair, I'm sure there are a million times more moments when he wants to wring mine.

We have problems like anyone else in a relationship.

However, there is something about seeing the father of your child with your child that makes him even more attractive.

When I watch him reading a book to our daughter, I just want to jump his bones. (Mentally, that is. Physically, I just want to sleep.)

I actually get tears in my eyes when I hear him making our daughter laugh.

My heart smiles when I see him reading her a book.

I love when he makes her giggle.

I love when my daughter asks, "Can we call Daddy?"

I love when she wants to help him cook.

I love when he puts our toddler on his shoulders and I walk beside them.

I like to spy on the two of them when he puts her to bed.

I like seeing them lie together. I like seeing my toddler put her head on the Fiancé's chest and snuggle.

I loved him as a person.

I love him even more as a father.

Part III
Bodily Functions

Grace: Look at my boobies!

Mom: Yes I see them.

Grace: I have small boobies.

Mom: Yeah, me too.

Grace: That's okay, Mommy, don't be sad. When you grow up you'll grow bigger boobies like me and we'll both have boobies together.

Mom: Really? That will be great!

Grace Purves-Ferguson, 2½, daughter of Sara Purves

The Toilet Hug

This is the most unromantic hug you'll ever give or receive, in the most unromantic setting, at the most unfortunate time. Your face hasn't been this close to a toilet bowl in a long, long time. And you're not even sick! Or hungover!

My daughter likes to go to the washroom . . . *on the toilet.*

I know. You're asking, "Isn't that a *good thing?*"

Well, yes . . . and no.

For many parents, the toddler's transition from diapers and Pull-Ups to Big Girl Underpants and Big Boy Underpants isn't easy. The son of one of my friends screams bloody murder every time he is told he has to go "potty" on the toilet.

One of my daughter's pre-school classmates was actually sent home because she had a "Number Two" accident in her underpants. And she wasn't sent home just for the day. She was told she was allowed to come back only when she was fully toilet trained.

I haven't seen my daughter's pre-school classmate in weeks. I suppose the toilet training isn't going so well, which is kind of unfortunate. I would hate to think that this little girl is going to miss an entire year of coloring, all because she wouldn't go potty on the toilet.

It may sound like I'm bragging because toilet training my toddler really wasn't all that painful. But I'm not. Whenever my friends ask me how I did it—how my daughter goes pee and poo on the toilet without screaming or throwing a temper tantrum—I just say, "I don't know. She just does. She just started doing it."

What I don't tell them, because all of them are so obsessed with getting their own children to use the washroom, is that sometimes the only thing worse than having your child still in diapers is having them toilet trained.

Yes, my daughter likes going to the washroom on the toilet. And yes, we've said goodbye to diapers.

My daughter also very much loves hugs.

But she likes to do both . . . at the same time.

You heard me. My toddler likes to hug me *while* she's on the toilet. You think changing a shitty diaper is disgusting? Well, my daughter may go Number Two on the toilet, but not only does she like to hug me while doing so, she actually *insists* on it.

Yes, my daughter is a rare breed known as the Toilet Hugger.

I know my daughter is a rare breed because I asked my friend, whose toddler is toilet trained, if her son ever makes her hug him when he goes to the washroom.

"Um, no," she responded, laughing. "He actually makes me leave the room."

Why can't I have her toddler?

I'm a firm believer, and always have been, that the washroom door should be shut when one goes to the potty, no matter what your age. I don't care if you've been married for twenty-five years. I still think the washroom door should be shut.

"You're so lucky," I moaned to my friend. "So he can wipe himself, too?"

"Oh, no," she said. "I still have to wipe him. He calls me back in when he's done."

Thank god. I would think life was really unfair if her toddler not only asked her to leave the room, but also knew how to wipe his own bum.

The point is, her toddler, unlike my toddler, asks his mother to *leave the room*. That's cool. He gets the concept of privacy. He has manners.

My daughter, once I place her on the toilet, scrunches her face until it turns red and announces, "It's coming! It's coming! It's coming!" and then says frantically, "Hug me! Hug me! Hug me!"

And, so, mostly because I love her, and also because her face looks so damn cute all red and flushed while she tries to push, I will hug her as, "It's coming! It's coming! It's coming!"

Without getting into too much detail, I just want you to imagine where my face is as I'm hugging my toddler while she's doing Number Two. Right. Exactly.

And one's face should *never* be that close to a toilet bowl unless one is puking after a night of drinking at a wicked party. Quite frankly, I haven't been so close to a toilet bowl in years. I miss those days. Sigh.

So, you see, dear parents, you may want to think twice about being so obsessed with getting your toddler out of diapers. You might just end up with a Toilet Hugger, like me.

Camel Bladders

Your toddler hasn't gone pee-pee in eighteen hours and you're thinking that this is what they call a "medical miracle." It's amazing that she can still hold it in. Until she can't. And you are nowhere near a toilet. This is why timing is everything when it comes to pee.

My daughter is like a camel.

The one thing that completely weirds me out about toddlers is their bladders. Take my daughter, for instance. My daughter is quite petite. (Of course she is. She's 3. But she is a petite 3-year-old.) Her bladder, I swear, must be the size of a peanut. Maybe an orange. And yet she can "hold it in" for eight hours.

I'm not sure how she does this. It's quite unbelievable.

Once, we left the house at 8 a.m., went to the airport, got on a plane, and four hours later landed at our destination. And the gal *still* didn't have to pee. (This only holds true, for some reason, during the day. You would be wrong to assume that just because your child holds it in for ten hours during the day, she will hold it in for ten hours during the night.)

The only problem is that when toddlers do have to pee, after holding it in for hours, they have to pee. They have to pee . . . *right now*.

I can't tell you how many times we've been in the car and suddenly I hear from the back seat, "Mommy, I have to pee."

"Of course you have to pee," you think to yourself. "It's been, like, ten hours!"

You then say, "Hold it in! Just hold it in! Hold it in!"

And they say, "But I have to pee, Mommy! I have to pee!"

See, when they don't need to pee—let's say when you're at home, where there are bathrooms on every floor—they can hold it in. But when you're on the highway, and you're lost, that's when they'll suddenly have to pee.

I can't tell you how many sudden stops I've made at Starbucks. I park the car illegally, then run in like a madwoman carrying my daughter and screaming, "Just hold it in! Just hold it in!" I usually manage to plop her on the toilet just before the waterfall pours out of her.

More than once, as we're making our way back to the car—with me all delighted that we made it "just in time"—I'll see a parking ticket on my windshield. These emergency washroom stops can be costly. I often wonder if I could fight the tickets: "My daughter had to pee, Your Honor! It was an emergency!"

They now have parking especially marked for expectant moms. There should be designated street parking for emergency washroom stops.

Once, I even had to stop at an outdoor shopping plaza. There was a doctor's office right beside a grungy Chinese food restaurant. I decided to take her into the doctor's office, the cleaner of the options.

The receptionist wasn't even at the desk, but I knew they had to have a washroom in there. And because my daughter "had to go pee," which I knew meant, "right now," I just walked through the hallways until I found it.

I try to explain to her—often—that she needs to tell me sooner than five seconds before she has to pee. I try to explain that there's a reason I always ask her if she wants to "try" before we leave the restaurant. I don't think she quite gets it just yet.

I figure toddlers can hold it in because they don't want to interrupt what they're doing to pee. Peeing to them, I figure, is kind of like chores for adults. We don't want to do them, but if we don't buy Tide, then we won't have clean clothes.

My toddler will also say things like, "I already peed this morning!"

And I'll say, "But it's 6 o'clock in the evening. You know, people pee four or five times a day! Sometimes more!" I try to make going to the washroom sound as fun as a trip for ice cream.

Toddlers haven't learned that going to the washroom isn't a bad thing. It's not a good thing, either. It's a nothing thing. It's just something that needs to be done. Like chores. Speaking of which, I need Tide.

Tampon Talk

Is it ever too early to talk about the birds and the bees?

As the mother of a toddler, you know that kids play with the darndest things.

They're less interested in the $50 "educational toy" you bought them from the "educational toy store" than the leaf they picked up in the backyard, or the feather from a dirty pigeon they found on the street.

Ever since my toddler was a baby, I've given her tampons to play with. I know, but talk about a fairly inexpensive toy! (Don't ask me how I know this, but tampons also make great toys for cats and puppies.) I think what gets my toddler's attention is that there are so many tampons in one box, and they're all the same. When she was really little, she liked to line them up. Now that she can actually speak, she asks for tampons to play with.

I'll be straightening my hair in the washroom and she'll open the cupboard under the sink and say, "I just need some tampons because I'm playing tea party and they have to come because they got an invitation."

Only the parent of a toddler can understand that it makes perfect sense for an almost-3-year-old to invite tampons to her tea party.

She was so into playing with tampons at one point, that whenever I went to the drugstore the thought actually crossed my mind that maybe I should by an extra box, just for my daughter.

And what better gift, really, than a gift I could actually use in the future?

And one day, in the middle of the month, it happened. I actually needed a tampon.

"Could you just open the door over there and grab me a tampon?" I asked my daughter. (My little slave.)

She complied and, without getting into too much detail, watched me do my thang. "Mommy," she asked, "what are you doing with the tampon?" (This coming from a girl who invites them to tea parties. What am *I* doing?)

I realized that I would need to have the tampon talk. But why exactly, and how exactly, do you have a tampon talk with a girl who isn't even 3, who doesn't remember to eat her pancakes unless you say, every forty-five seconds, "Eat your pancakes!"?

"They're for big people," I told her. And left it at that.

I have this memory of being in a grocery story with my mother when I was about 7, asking her why she was buying a big box of maxi-pads. "They're maxi-pads," she told me. To which I asked, "What are they for?" To which my mother said, "I'll tell you when we get home." To which I asked, "Why can't you tell me now?" To which she said, "I'll tell you at home," and rushed me out. I don't think she told me. At least not that day.

Like my mother did so long ago, I managed to escape the tampon talk—at least for that day. But the problem doesn't exactly go away. In addition to playing with tampons, my daughter now also likes to give them out to everyone. Once she handed one to my father. "I don't think I'll be needing that," he said. He was embarrassed, sort of in the same way my mother was embarrassed when she was doing my daughter's laundry one day at her house (don't ask, please don't ask) and came across one of my pairs of underwear.

"These are yours, I assume," my mother said, handing over a thong. "They're very small."

It would be one thing if my daughter kept her tampon fascination at home, but no such luck. When we're in public bathroom stalls, she will always point to the tampon/maxi-pad disposal and ask, "What's this for?"

To which I yell, "DO NOT TOUCH THAT!!!" Then I'll say, in a gentler voice, "It's for tampons."

Now every time we're in a public washroom stall, she'll point at the disposal and yell, "That's for tampons!"

And I'll yell, "DO NOT TOUCH THAT!"

God only knows what the women in stalls next to us think about my daughter saying, in her cute little baby voice, "That's for tampons. Right, Mommy? That's for tampons."

And one day, she'll want to know more about tampons, and I'll really have to explain all about the menstrual cycle. I'm not really looking forward to that day, but I'll deal with it.

I'll deal with it, too, when I have to seriously answer the vagina question. I know of a toddler who loves looking at her mom's vagina. "What's that thing?" she'll ask her mother. "Why is there hair?" My daughter has done the exact same thing, and for now, I've got it covered.

For what it's worth, I'm less scared of talking about bras. I mean, Baby Gap sells bras for 4-year-olds. They wear them as undershirts now. And I kind of think it's adorable when my daughter says, "I want to help you put on your bra," and will slip my arms through the straps. She gets the idea of boobs.

These are the things that parents of girls will have to deal with. Pretty bad, I know, but I think you're worse off if you have a son. One of my friends was telling me about how she came home one day to see her 5-year-old masturbating on the couch. She doesn't think he really knew what he was doing, just that touching his penis felt good.

"I would have died," I told her. "I would have died! What did you do?"

"I just let him continue," she said, "and I went upstairs."

I don't know. Suddenly, inviting tampons to a tea party doesn't seem so bad.

Regression

They say toddlers make you young again. They also make you rude again. What happened to your social graces?

I burped out loud the other day at my friend's house. He had just made me a lovely dinner of orange chicken and roasted potatoes.

"Squeeze me," I said, covering my mouth.

"Oh, come on!" he said. "That's disgusting. And what did you just say?"

"I said, 'Squeeze me,' like 'Excuse me,'" I exclaimed, then sheepishly added, "Sorry! I couldn't help it. It just came out."

And I really couldn't help it. The burp really did just come out. My toddler burps all the time after she eats (and sometimes just for fun).

Lately, I've realized that, because of living with my toddler, I'm actually regressing into a very uncouth woman. I may even need to be sent to a finishing school.

I knew I'd hit rock bottom the day I was at another friend's house for dinner. (There's a big plus when you don't know how to cook, which is that others have to cook for you.) We were just sitting there talking when I said, "I have to poo."

"Oh, come on! Is that really necessary? I don't need to hear that," she moaned.

"I'm sorry! It's just that my daughter says it all the time! I think I'm learning from her."

I've realized that other mothers of toddlers also seem to regress, and not just when they're talking about bodily functions. These mothers will do things to you that no one else would ever do—unless they, too, were the mother of a toddler. They might, for example, wipe a crumb off your cheek.

Not so long ago, I was talking to another mother on the street, a woman I didn't know well at all. Suddenly she was wiping my cheek!

I jumped back in shock. I'm not used to people I barely know touching my cheek. "Was there a bug or something?" I asked. Because that's the only reason I could think of for this woman to be touching my face.

"No, just a crumb. Don't worry," she said knowingly, "I got it."

I should thank god she didn't pull out a tissue, lick it, and *then* wipe my mouth. Or start checking my hair for lice. Or start picking my nose (my toddler does this to perfect strangers).

Other mothers of toddlers have found themselves in boardrooms at work asking grown colleagues—some of them CEOs!—"Do you want to go to lunch? It's lunchtime! Let's have lunch!" as if they were talking to their 2-year-old instead of a 56-year-old man in a suit who runs a multimillion-dollar company.

If you're one of these mothers (and admit it, you are!), you may find yourself putting your hand on someone's forehead when they tell you they think they're coming down with something. They might have a fever!

You find yourself telling friends that you're using baby shampoo these days, and that you never realized how nice it is! You eat mac and cheese—and really love it—even though you haven't had mac and cheese since first-year university.

You start walking around with kids' Band-Aids on your elbows.

And you get angry with people who don't use "the magic words" after they ask you for something or you give them something.

You basically turn into a toddler yourself.

And, squeeze me, is it just me or does everything really taste better with the crusts cut off?

Part IV
Is This the Little Girl I Carried?

Mommy: Your daycare teacher said that a little boy showed you his penis today?
Ginette: Yes, I saw his penis, but that's okay. I didn't mind.

Ginette Mazerolle, 4, daughter of Marisol Rocha

Worth Every Penny

These are those American Express/Hallmark moments when certain things your toddler says to you really are priceless.

There are times when you think you couldn't possibly love your toddler more than you do *at this exact moment.*

For me, one of those moments happened outside a water fountain in a park near our house. When she was a baby, my daughter used to love throwing pennies or stones in this fountain. And now that she can talk, she likes to make wishes before she throws something in.

She likes it when I go first. On this one day, I threw in my penny and said, "I wish that Rowan will have a very happy day."

"Mommy, you always say that," she said.

"But it's true. I do! I wish that you always have happy days," I told her.

Then I gave her a penny to toss in and told her to make a wish.

"I wish I could be with Mommy forever and ever," she said and then tossed her penny in.

I honestly felt tears well up in my eyes and my throat get thick as honey. I could barely swallow. It was by far the nicest thing anyone has ever said to or about me.

I have never loved my toddler more than at that exact moment. What a good girl! What a nice girl to say that she wished she could be with her "Mommy forever and ever." I was a friggin' fantastic mother! She was a friggin' fantastic daughter!

The next day, I couldn't wait to go back to the fountain. I wanted that rush of love all over again.

I threw in my penny.

"I wish that Rowan will have a very happy day," I said as we stood before the fountain.

"Mommy, you always say that," my daughter told me again.

"But it's true! I do! I wish that you always have happy days," I said.

I handed her a penny. I couldn't wait to feel my heart swell again. I couldn't wait to hear those words come from my daughter's mouth—my daughter who clearly loves me more than any other human in the entire universe! I couldn't wait to hear that she wanted to be with "Mommy forever and ever."

I was already smiling, blinking back tears! I knew what was coming. I was a good mother! How could I not be when my daughter's wish was to be with me not just forever, but forever and *ever*? She really did appreciate everything I do for her! Her wish was to be with me forever and ever.

I am such hot shit, I thought to myself.

"Are you ready to make your wish?" I asked my daughter.

"Yes," she said, throwing in her penny. "I wish I could go to Disneyland."

Doh!

First Comes Lub

You think your toddler's first crush is super-adorable, even though you'd never peg her as being into that type of guy (usually at least two decades older). If she wasn't 2, you'd definitely disapprove.

Nanny Mimi told me about my daughter's first crush. I was a little concerned, like any parent would be upon finding out her 2-year-old has a crush on a much, much older man.

My toddler's crush was—gaa!—my age (30-muffle-muffle).

That's a couple of *decades* older than the man I'd ideally like my toddler to have a crush on. (Personally, I've always thought the ideal age difference between a man and a woman is eight years, if the woman is over 25. I don't know why. I just do.)

Anyway, Nanny Mimi told me my daughter was "madly in love" with Hulgar, the instructor at her twice-weekly morning music classes. I was embarrassed to learn that, at the end of the most recent class, my 2-year-old invited Hulgar to "come over and play at my house and then sleep over."

It's going to be a while—or never—before I allow my daughter to ask a man to sleep over, at least without asking my permission first. I'm all for women's liberation, and I don't think it's a bad thing for a girl to ask a boy out. I just think, perhaps, that before asking an older man to sleep over, my daughter should at least share a package of animal crackers with him.

Call me a prude.

As soon as I found out that my daughter was "madly in love," of course I had to check out this Hulgar. I cleared my schedule.

I wanted to know what kind of man my daughter was into.

Would he be tall, dark and handsome? Would he be blonde and blue-eyed? Did he know how to treat a woman with respect? Did he treat his mother well? Did he have a good sense of humor? Did he open the car door?

These are all the qualities I hoped—one day—my daughter would look for in a man. I just never expected her to have a crush so soon after coming out of my womb! She was still in diapers. It was too soon. Too, too soon.

I went to the next music class to check out this Hulgar who had stolen my daughter's heart, a man my daughter liked so much she had invited him to spend the night.

He was not what I expected, looks-wise. It's not that he wasn't handsome. I just never expected that this somewhat shy, quiet and reserved man would be my toddler's type. Not that she should have a "type" at age 2.

My daughter immediately wanted to sit next to Hulgar when we walked into the room. But—and I felt bad about this—she had some stiff competition. There were a lot of other females, between the ages of 6 months and 3 years, who all apparently had crushes on Hulgar, the Music Teacher, and were vying for his attention.

These females, in their fresh diapers, pretty sundresses and hair bows, seemed to know how to flirt a lot better than my still-bald toddler, who was wearing a sweat suit, and who blushed and buried her head in my lap every time Hulgar came close.

Some of the little girls, who weren't even walking yet, knew how to bat their eyelashes coyly. Some of them even did the whole, "Oops! I dropped my tambourine, silly me!" shtick, and waited for Hulgar to come around and pick up their instruments. Smart little flirts!

I kind of got my daughter's attraction, once Hulgar started to play his guitar and sing. What girl doesn't swoon a little when listening to a man sing and play the guitar for her, even if that song is "Ring Around the Rosie?"

I'm not sure, though, that 2-year-olds get the concept of crushes. Thank god. At least my daughter won't be waiting by her banana phone for his call, or taking baths, without water, in case Hulgar called and she couldn't hear the phone ring.

She won't complain to her other pint-size friends that he's hot with her one minute and cold with her the next and wondering if he really likes her and asking me pressing questions like, "He said he was only meeting his ex-girlfriend for coffee. Should I be concerned?" She won't be wondering if he is gay or just a really good dresser. That time will come soon enough.

For weeks after that music class, whenever I'd mention Hulgar's name, my daughter would blush and get all shy. I was not exactly a nice, understanding mother during this time.

I would ask her, "Do you love Hulgar?"

"I lub Hulgar," she'd say.

I would walk around the house, twelve times a day, singing, "Rowan and Hulgar sitting on a tree. K-I-S-S-I-N-G. First comes love, then comes marriage, then comes Rowan and Hulgar pushing a baby carriage." I wanted to see her get all shy and blush. It was funny.

In fact, I sang it so many times that my daughter would join in. If I even dared change Hulgar's name in the song, to, let's say "Zen" (who is a boy Rowan's age), she'd get pissed off at me.

"Hulgar!" she'd scream. "Hulgar and Rowan pushing a baby carriage! Not Zen and Rowan!"

Music class ended but my daughter's crush didn't exactly go away. "When are we going to see Hulgar again?" she'd ask occasionally. "I lub Hulgar."

One of my friend's sons, who is 3, has a crush (luckily for my friend on a girl just two months older than him). He calls his crush his "wife."

I think her toddler is a very courageous boy to announce that another little girl is his "wife," before even offering up one of his toy drawers for her "things" or knowing her favorite color. He just blushes and asks for his "wife" to come over all the time. And like most guys, his crush sometimes annoys him. "My wife doesn't pick up toys!" he once announced. (Why do I have a feeling this boy will turn into a man who says, "My wife doesn't pick up her wet towels off the bed"?)

A few weeks after music class ended, my daughter's crush on Hulgar was over. Time does heal all wounds and my toddler had moved on. Eventually, she even had a new crush. Fickle girl.

This time the crush was on her JK teacher, and this time, my daughter actually seemed to understand that having a crush can be embarrassing and not necessarily an easy thing to admit. This crush hit her hard . . . and fast.

I swear, once she started having a crush on her JK teacher—after *two days* of school—she stopped eating as many pieces of the pancakes I cut up for her each morning before heading to school, like an adult female who really likes someone and whose stomach is in a constant knot.

Two days—yes, only 48 hours—after school began my toddler said to me out of the blue, "Mommy, I lub Sean Lamb. But don't tell anybody, okay?"

"Okay," I promised. "I won't tell anybody that you love Sean Lamb."

"Don't tell anybody," she said again. "Okay?"

I was thrilled that my daughter felt enough confidence in me to confess that she had a crush on a man she'd known for less time than it takes fresh flowers to die. I was her confidant! I loved it. This was exactly how I wanted our mother/daughter relationship to be. But I can't keep secrets very well.

I couldn't help but tell everybody, including friends, my parents and the Fiancé. I mean, when your kid says something that cute, you have to tell the world.

"Guess what my daughter told me today? She said, 'I love Sean Lamb,' her teacher! *And* then she told me that I couldn't tell anyone." I blabbed this to everyone. Everyone.

My toddler had matured, though, since her crush on Hulgar, the Music Teacher. She wouldn't let me sing, "Sean and Rowan sitting on a tree. K-I-S-S-I-N-G!" She'd just be all, like, "Don't tell anyone, Mommy!" and give me a look of mortification. She was actually self-conscious. I could tell she regretted ever mentioning anything about "lubbing" Sean.

A couple of months into the school year, I asked her if she still was "in love" with Sean Lamb.

"No," she answered. "He can be a grumpy-pants."

My daughter is learning—quickly, it seems—that men are moody creatures.

But that's okay. I'm sure her disappointment in her JK teacher won't matter in a few months anyway. She'll likely be into tattoo bikers by then and she won't tell me anything.

Copycats

Imitation is supposedly the sincerest form of flattery. But that doesn't mean we want our boys to wear nail polish. And should any 3-year-old really be wearing heels?

Fred's mother, my friend, likes to wear red nail polish. So does Fred. He's 3. Yesterday when I saw him at a party, I noticed that he was really party-ready.

Because my friend had been painting her fingernails red, before they left the house, Fred also wanted red nail polish. His nails looked good. My friend had done a nice job.

But hopefully, and not because I think there's anything wrong with an adult man who sports red nail polish, he'll grow out of this phase of wanting to be just like his mother. It might be easier on him in his teenage years.

I'm pretty sure my friend feels the same way. She thought it was painful to have her son copy her by wearing red nail polish. Unfortunately, though, she couldn't see a way out. "He had a fit. I had to put it on him," she moaned at the party. "I had to! He wouldn't stop crying until I put it on!"

What's even more painful is to watch my daughter walk in my heels. It's downright dangerous. Sometimes I can barely walk in heels. Yet there she is, trotting around the house in six-inch heels that are five sizes too big. I keep thinking, "Okay, I'll just tell the doctor in emergency that she was wearing my shoes and that's why her ankle is broken. They can't send me to jail for that, right?"

My daughter also likes to wear deodorant, which would be fine if she had the motor skills required to actually get the deodorant under her armpits, which she does not. She has the motor skills required to simply put a white stripe across whatever shirt she is wearing (thereby offering solid proof that even deodorants that promise to be invisible are so not invisible).

"I want to wear deodorant, too!" she'll demand.

"But you don't need it! It's for big people!" I'll tell her.

"I am a big person," she'll say.

The point is, toddlers are copycats. They want to do exactly what you do, and they want to wear exactly what you have on.

My daughter also wants my diamond earrings. "Mommy, can we share them?" she'll ask.

"But you don't even have your ears pierced," I'll say, as if that should be the end of the conversation.

"I want diamond earrings, too!" she'll demand.

I want to tell her that she can't just get diamond earrings (although I am pleased with her taste). How could I explain how hard I worked for those diamond earrings—the pain and heartache I suffered to get those diamond earrings? (And, by the way, what I had to go through were a number of unemployed boyfriends, and even one pot-dealer ex, who you'd think would have money, but actually spent all of it on drugs for himself. Needless to say, he still lived in his parents' basement and I wasn't going to see anything sparkly other than a bong the sunlight was hitting at exactly the right angle.) Yes, I had to go through a lot before I found the perfect man who had a job, was good at his job, and thought I was worthy, one birthday, of diamond earrings.

I'm lucky I don't wear makeup and don't own much of it. I have friends whose toddlers insist on wearing lipstick and blush.

I do, however, own a few items of clothing that I truly love. And it's always these pieces of clothing my daughter wants to wear, like my Paul Smith scarf.

"We can share it, Mommy," she'll say.

I'm happy that she gets the concept of sharing. At the same time, though, I want to say, "No, it's mine!"

Usually, though, I end up letting her try it on. I know that one day, when she's older, I'll probably want to borrow her things. I just hope we end up having the same shoe size.

Baby Breath

Your toddler is an actual human being and has adult-strength bad breath to prove it. You realize that, for the first time, you don't want to snuggle. Do they make child-friendly Listerine?

My relationship with my daughter changed this morning. We reached a new plateau. And there's no turning back.

In all relationships there comes a time when things change. Like when you've been dating a guy for a few months, and you've had wicked sex each and every time you've seen him, and then there's that first night you sleep together but you don't have sex. You know your relationship has changed.

Or when you're dating a guy and all along he's been making you romantic dinners, with candles, and then, one time, you have a really bad stomachache and he asks you if you want him to run out and get you some Pepto-Bismol. You know your relationship has changed.

The romance is dead. And there's no turning back.

As adults, we call this "getting comfortable" with someone. It's inevitable.

Well, this morning, I guess I "got comfortable" with my daughter. I woke up with her snuggling next to me and I immediately smiled. She's so warm and cozy in the mornings! She's always a little sweaty and her hair looks like a mop. It's adorable. But, this morning, something was different.

This morning, she opened her mouth and I couldn't believe it! My toddler, for the first time in her life, had halitosis. She had bad breath!

Gone was the sweet baby breath. She had full-on, adult-bad, you-need-to-brush-your-teeth breath. I held my head back.

It was the first time I realized that my toddler was an actual person! And once you come to that realization (and smell your daughter's bad breath), you know your relationship has changed. Our romance, in a way, was dead.

I was telling my friend about this when she said her husband recently picked up their 8-year-old son only to realize, for the first time, that he had B.O.

One day I'm going to have a daughter with B.O.

I can get over this. It's like the time in high school when I had the boyfriend who wore the same smelly sweater for six days in a row. I got over it because I was madly in love with him. And once the initial shock that Rowan is a human being (with bad breath!) wears off, I'm sure I'll get over this, too. Because I'm madly in love with her. And of course she has bad breath! I have bad breath! (Of course, the Queen poos! Even Gwyneth Paltrow poos!)

It was just sad. Like the first time your child ignores you during a play date. You know she no longer needs you as much, and that's sad. It means she's growing up. Well, baby bad breath makes you realize the same thing (and that maybe someone should come up with baby mouthwash).

It's also sad because once your child has bad breath you realize you really have to make more of an effort to brush her teeth. (We've been bad at that, I'll admit. I have one friend who started brushing her baby's teeth when there was only one tooth to brush.)

Brushing toddlers' teeth is like working your way through a maze. You're not sure how you're going to get through it, but you know you have to.

"NO! Stop sucking on the toothbrush. You can't suck on it. Open up! No! Open! Stop Sucking! No. Fine. Screw this."

Come to think of it, maybe a little case of halitosis isn't so bad.

Will Maddy Be Wearing Rain Boots?

Be forewarned: Your toddler actually notices what other kids are wearing (or not wearing) and it matters.

My daughter is only a toddler, but she's already a teenager in some ways.

I'll never forget someone telling me that after you give birth, you are not only raising a baby/toddler/child, but one day you'll be raising a teenager. That realization—that one day I'd have a sexually active teenager who just might want to try drugs—scared the crap out of me. But I thought I had some time. I didn't realize the transition to teenagehood would happen so fast.

Don't worry. My daughter is not making pot cookies or drinking vodka underage in someone's basement out of a sippy cup or stealing my car to drive to New Orleans or getting felt up at overnight camp. (Not that I did any of that. I swear.)

But she is already insecure in a way that I think only females can be when they hit the teenage years. This breaks my heart. I thought I'd have at least until she was 11 before she wanted to wear certain clothes that were in vogue for her generation.

Nope. Ever since she started hanging with other children her age, Rowan wants to wear what they wear.

And I'm really not opposed to this. I'm not the kind of parent—at least not yet—who ever says, "Well, if your best friend jumped off a bridge onto a highway, would you do the same thing?"

I'm more like, "Okay, my daughter will wear only dresses because her best friend in pre-school wears dresses, so I'll get her dresses." I do, however, find it very sad that peer pressure doesn't wait for the teen years. These days, it hits toddlers.

The other day it was raining. I told my daughter to go put on her rain boots.

"Will Maddy be wearing rain boots to school today?" my daughter asked me. I said that, yes, I thought Maddy would be wearing rain boots.

"Are you sure Maddy will be wearing rain boots, too?" she asked.

"Yes, I'm sure Maddy will be wearing rain boots," I told her. So she got her rain boots on.

That one question—"Will Maddy be wearing rain boots?"—brought back every memory of me begging my parents to buy me the same clothes my friends wore.

I grew up as a child in the 80s, so I'm loath to tell you what I needed to wear in order to feel like I fit in. Did I really beg my mother for safety pins to pin my pants? Seriously, did I really beg for fluorescent pink leg warmers? Alas, I did.

The point, however, isn't my bad fashion sense. It's that I remember the feeling of not fitting in and wanting to. I remember what it was like to think that just the right pair of pants would make all the difference in the world. I don't want Rowan to feel like that. Ever.

The Fiancé believes we shouldn't give in to our toddler's every desire. He doesn't get why I went to five Gaps across the city to find the same hat that my toddler's friend, Rebecca, owned.

But I know the Fiancé just doesn't get what it's like to be a girl. It's not fashion magazines that are to blame for making us want certain clothes. I think it's in our DNA to want to dress like our friends, and to ask if Maddy will be wearing rain boots. It has to be. My toddler doesn't read magazines.

And really, to dress like our friends is easy enough.

But then there are the times she just wants to *do* exactly what her friends do or have done. One of her pre-school classmates—

one of her "besties"—was taking a week off school to go to Sweden for a relative's wedding. For the entire week, all my toddler said to me was, "I want to go to Sweden. I want to go to Sweden like Kai." She wouldn't shut up about going to Sweden.

And while I may be the type of mother who will drive around all afternoon to five Gaps until I find the exact right polka-dotted hat, I'm certainly not enough of a pushover to get on a plane and fly to Sweden just because one of her friends went.

Instead, I took my daughter to a park we'd never visited.

"We're in Sweden!" I told her.

"This is Sweden?" she asked.

"Yup. This is Sweden," I announced. "We're here!"

"Now I've been to Sweden, too," she said. "I'm going to tell Kai."

Since then, I've started practicing, "If all of your friends jumped off a bridge onto a highway, would you?" I figure I'd better get ready, because one day, I won't be able to trick her into thinking a park is Sweden.

But for now, at least, we have the polka-dotted hat—the hat that cost me more money in gas than it did on the price tag. But that's okay. The hat can keep us warm in "Sweden."

Part V
Little Einsteins . . . Or Maybe Not

Regan: I want to go to 'chool, Mommy!

Mommy: It's Good Friday, there's no school today.

Regan: Why's it good, Mommy?

Mommy: Don't you know the Easter story?

Regan: About the Easter bunny?

Mommy: No . . . about Jesus. Do you know who Jesus is?

Regan: No, Mommy.

Mommy: Well, I'll have to get some stories about him and read them to you.

Regan: (excited, and running from room): I'll get my Dora book! It has LOTS of stories. Maybe there's one about Dora and Jesus.

Regan Carruthers, 3½, daughter of Sarah Macey

Practice Doesn't Make Perfect

You've been doing it night after night, week after week, month after month, and it still takes you an hour and a half to get your toddler into one pajama leg.

Toddlers are good at a lot of things. They are good at taking up every free minute of your time. They are good at destroying things. They are good at playing with plastic cups. They are not good, however, at getting into their pajamas.

You honestly can't help but start to think that something is *wrong* with your toddler when you try to get her into her pajamas.

It's during the getting-ready-for-bedtime when you really realize that you are so not raising a Little Einstein and that maybe you should get her *checked out by a professional*.

I'm not exaggerating when I say I could get on a plane and fly to Maui in the time it takes to get both my daughter's legs into her pajama bottoms.

I'm pretty positive that in the amount of time it takes to get both legs into her pajama bottoms and her pajama shirt on properly, not only could I fly to Maui, but also I could get some pretty damn good tan lines as well.

It's not so difficult to get her into her bedroom, which is the first step in the long process of getting her dressed for bed. I'm all about trickery. "Race you!" I'll say, and then we'll run up the stairs. Of course, I let her beat me.

I'm a competitive person by nature (even with my offspring), but I'll give up winning the race up the stairs if it means it'll get her into her bedroom.

Usually, things go horribly wrong once we're in the room.

There comes a point when a toddler is old enough to pick out what she wants to wear to bed, but not old enough to actually get into the sleepwear herself. And this is where the three-hour process—or what seems more like six hours—really begins.

It starts with trying to get your toddler naked. Usually, I turn this into a game. What else can you call it when your toddler is jumping on the bed at the same time as you're trying to pull off her pants and shirt? So we call it a game. She jumps on the bed and falls. While she is briefly down for the count, I grab her pants and pull them off. She starts jumping on the bed again, and when she's down for the count for the second time, I go in and whip her shirt over her head. And then I have a naked toddler, jumping on the bed.

I'm pretty proud of myself at this stage. Exhausted, yes, but baby-steps have been made toward getting her bedtime-ready. She's at least naked.

Which is when the second game starts. The game is called "Naked Toddler Jumping on the Bed." I know, unique. This is when she usually suggests that we have a pillow fight. It is also the part where I begin the process of bribing. I'm all for the bribe. We'll have a pillow fight *after* you get into your pajamas, I tell her, "but first you have to pick out your pajamas."

I know. You're asking, why don't you just pick them out for her? Well, I would, if I knew it wouldn't lead to a fit of, "I don't want to wear those! They don't match." I can't guarantee that this won't happen even if I do let her pick, but I can pretty much guarantee that she will throw a fit if she doesn't. "Go pick them out now," I say.

And she'll trudge over to her pajama drawer and pick out a shirt with pink and purple hearts and a pair of shorts with brown and blue cows on them. (Sure, honey, that matches.)

This is the part when it gets really tricky. It's not that she's running around (with me chasing after her) with her pink-and-purple-heart shirt and brown-and-blue-cow bottoms, it's just that getting her into them is as difficult as math class was to me in Grade 9 (I passed . . . with 51 percent . . . and I had a private tutor).

First, the Pull-Ups must go on. This is accomplished by sitting on the floor, throwing her over my shoulder and somehow managing to slide them up her kicking legs. That's the easy part.

Putting on the pajama bottoms is when things get really difficult.

"Okay, stand still," I say. "Now, put your leg in."

And she will.

"Now, put your other leg in the other hole," I tell her.

And while she's putting her other leg in, the first leg somehow manages to get out of the leg hole *we had just got it into*. It happens so quickly, like seeing a spider on a wall and by the time you get a shoe to crush it, it's gone.

"Okay, let's put the other leg in," I say, back to square one. Ten minutes later, I sound like a crazy person.

"No, not that leg. The other leg. No, not that leg. The other leg. Yes, you got it. Now the other leg! No, that other leg! No, not that one. The other leg! The other one! Yes, that leg. No, not that leg. That leg! Yes, yes! No! Wait! No, yes, wait, no. Argh! Let's start again!"

I find myself saying, "No, the other leg! Not that one! The other one! No, the other one! THE OTHER ONE!" about a thousand times before we actually get both legs into the right leg holes.

Sometimes, both legs end up in the same pant leg, making her look like a mermaid. Which only makes matter worse, because my toddler, at present, is obsessed with mermaids and somehow thinks that she could go to sleep like this, with both legs in the same leg hole.

I end up thinking to myself, "Could she just go to sleep with both legs in the same leg hole? Maybe she could. Could she?"

The answer, of course, is "No!" I know she'll be calling out for me in two minutes, screaming, "I can't move my legs!"

Finally—finally—when both legs are in the right pant hole, and she's half-dressed for bed, it's time to put on the shirt.

Sometimes, I actually find myself sweating throughout this process, because getting a toddler into pajamas is kind of like an aerobic workout. I sometimes think I need a steam bath afterward to relax.

Most likely, at this point, she's back to jumping on the bed and I just whip her shirt on over her head. She's at the stage in her life where she can find the armholes herself. Sort of. Well, she can usually manage to find one armhole. (This is the point where I clap and scream, "Yay! You did it!" You know, that whole positive reinforcement thing.)

But by the time she attempts to put her other arm through the other armhole, she usually misses and puts her arm through the neck hole.

"That's the neck hole," I scream. She laughs.

"Like this?" she'll ask, with her arm and neck through the neck hole.

"No, not like that!" I'll say.

Which, again, she thinks is just hilarious. I just look at her like she's crazy and help her put her arm back through the neck hole and into the armhole. And voila! After what seems like an all-day exam, she's finally into her freaking pajamas.

Sure, you say, you said earlier that you could fly to Maui in less time than it takes to get your toddler to bed. Well, getting the toddler into the pajamas is only the start of the process. The rest includes her needing the right two pillows, the strategic placement of a blanket, the location of that night's chosen stuffed animal, a sippy cup of water and many goodnight hugs and kisses.

Each and every night, we go through the same routine. Which is why I think sometimes that my toddler may be a little *slow*. Shouldn't she understand by now that there are two leg holes?

The point is this: Whether you have a boy or a girl, you should buy only nightgowns. It will cut at least two hours off the bedtime routine.

Little Litigators

You're going to find yourself in ridiculous arguments with your toddler over numbers and time. They're definitely not smart enough to go to law school. Not that you're worried about that. Yet.

Admit it. We all hope our toddlers end up as successful and productive members of society. Sure, we wish them happiness and health as well, but once your toddler starts talking and can actually understand small concepts, like, "Do you want a carrot?" you can't help but ask the question, "What do you want to be when you grow up?"

It's a typical question, along with, "How old are you?" and "What's your favorite color?"

The first time I asked my daughter what she wanted to be when she grew up, she answered very confidently, "A garbage truck driver."

I was like, dude, where did that come from?

I suppose "garbage," "truck" and "driver" were three words she could pronounce. I think I even told her that the politically correct term for "garbage truck driver" was "sanitation employee."

Of course, she couldn't pronounce "sanitation employee."

Not that it mattered, anyway. She just yelled at me, "I want to be a garbage truck driver!"

She actually got quite pissy. She didn't want to be a "sanitation employee." She wanted to be a "garbage truck driver."

Which is cool. Sometimes I find myself walking briskly down the street, trying to outwalk my racing brain, which is full of questions like, "Why did I ever want to be a writer? How did I end up here? Why aren't I in an office fixing someone's teeth?" Then I'll look at sanitation employees—rather, garbage truck drivers—and think to myself, "They get to be out in the fresh air (minus the smell of garbage around them), they probably don't have to work that many hours, they probably get paid well, and they probably don't lie in bed at night freaking out about their jobs, like I do."

Anyway, that dream of my daughter's didn't last long. A few months later, I asked her again what she wanted to be when she grew up. She said, "A race car driver," which I thought was really cool, although I have no idea where that came from either.

Toddlers never say they want to do what their parents do for a living. Which is good, at least on my end. That's because I know what it's like to be a writer, and I wouldn't wish the emotional baggage that comes along with being a writer on my worst enemy. (Okay, maybe on my worst enemy. I'd want them to have the never-ending pressure of deadlines, and coming up with story ideas, and that awful feeling of walking into a bookstore to see thousands of other books, and thinking, "Why would anyone buy mine?")

The Fiancé, on the other hand, is a lawyer. Like me, he often complains about his job (but not nearly as much). Because the difference between being a partner at a law firm and being a self-employed writer is that partners at law firms make a heck of a lot more money, and law firms have their own cafeterias, which self-employed writers do not. We just have kitchens, and my kitchen cupboards and refrigerator are always empty. Most of the time, I literally am a starving writer.

In any case, I wouldn't mind if my daughter became a lawyer.

However, at the rate we're going, my toddler is not going to be a lawyer, or at least not a lawyer in any courtroom.

She's the single worst negotiator I have ever witnessed.

She likes sitting on the toilet a lot. Don't ask me why. I mean, you can ask, but I wouldn't have an answer for you. She just does. She can sit there for an hour.

"I think you're done," I'll say to her, after we've been sitting there for fifteen minutes and both the pee and the poo have already come out.

"No, it's coming in five more minutes," she'll tell me.

"No, it's not," I'll say. "You're done."

"Five more minutes," she'll say.

"How about three more minutes," I'll say. Hanging out in washrooms is boring.

"How about one more minute," she'll ask, and I'll wonder how we got into haggling over the amount of time she's allowed to sit on the toilet, like I'm haggling for five dollars less on a handbag at a flea market.

"How about zero more minutes," I'll say.

And she'll say "okay," and get off the toilet.

See? She's a bad negotiator.

My friend's son is a two-minute litigator. He's always saying, "In two more minutes," about everything.

"It's time to go to bed," my friend will say to him.

"In two more minutes," he'll say.

"It's time to go eat dinner."

"In two more minutes," he'll say.

"It's time to wash your hands."

"In two more minutes," he'll say.

I have another friend whose daughter is a three-minute litigator. She always says, "In three more minutes."

My friend actually bought an alarm clock, which she sets every time her daughter says, "In three more minutes" so she can have proof that three minutes have gone by. Because, let's face it, toddlers don't understand time and three minutes to them is really three months in adult land.

My daughter is the worst negotiator when it comes to reading books at bedtime. "I want you to read me ten books tonight," she'll say, to which I'll laugh loudly in her face and say, "No way that's happening! I'll read you four books."

"I want eleven books," she'll say. Again, I'll laugh, "Are you crazy? You're crazy! You ain't getting eleven books."

"How about three books?" she'll say.

See? She's just plain bad at negotiating. Or she's just really bad at numbers, which doesn't bode well for a career in accounting either.

"Okay, you win. Three books it is," I'll say, making as if I'm giving in to something really big.

I wonder if you have to be good at numbers to be a sanitation employee or a race car driver.

Art Schmart

Is a feather on a napkin really considered art? And what does a mother do with all the "art" her toddler brings home (while coping with her guilt over the 739 trees that have been cut down during its creation)?

Grown-ups often get into a pseudo-intellectual debate over what constitutes art. And it's not uncommon, when gallery hopping, or attending art exhibits, to mutter under your breath, "My kid can do that! Why is *that* worth $200,000?"

Well, I can assure you that my toddler does do art. And a hell of a lot of it.

On my fridge right now is a sheet of white paper with a pink feather, a googly eye, and two pompoms glued on. Genius. There's also half of a paper plate with different-colored tissue paper stuck to it. Genius! There's another piece of blue construction paper with scribbles all over it and a final piece of red construction paper with my daughter's handprint. That was from her first day of school. (I don't know exactly why they call school for toddlers "school." All they do, it seems, is a heck of a lot of coloring and gluing.)

My daughter comes home from pre-school sometimes with five pieces of "artwork" in her knapsack. And by artwork, I mean scribbles all over pieces of paper ripped from a coloring book. I have stacks of sheets of paper with scribbles all over them in every room of the house.

I like the fact my daughter loves arts and crafts. The world needs artists. But it's gotten to the point where every spare counter-top, every bookshelf, every coffee table, in my home, is covered with piles of her "artwork."

Let's do the math. Five pieces of "art" a day, five days a week, equals twenty-five pieces of paper. Twenty-five pieces a paper, times four weeks in every month, equals 100 pieces of paper. One hundred times ten, for each month of school a year, equals 1,000. Yup, that's kind of what it feels like, too. It feels like there are a thousand pieces of paper (it's art!) lying around the house.

If my toddler continues this way, for even three more years, and I keep everything she makes at school, along with all the "art" she makes at home, I'll have more than 3,000 pieces of paper in my house.

Aside from renting a storage locker, what's a mother supposed to do with all this "art?" What do you do with all the paper plates with tissue paper glued on that your own kid made, sometimes saying to you as they hand it over, "I made it just for you, Mom! I made it just for you!"

It's so sweet knowing your toddler made something, "just for you."

I feel awfully guilty when I open the trash and throw her "art" out.

But I have to. There's just no room, even for the art she's made "especially for me."

"You're only supposed to keep the ones that are especially meaningful," my friend, who has four children under the age of 8, told me.

"But how do you know if it's especially meaningful?" I asked her.

"You know, the ones where they write, 'My favorite color is red,'" my friend answered.

Apparently, my friend and I have two very different views on what constitutes "especially meaningful" when it comes to toddler "art."

I have a feeling this friend has closets upon closets full of "especially meaningful" works of art by her children.

After being handed the 797th piece of artwork, nothing really is that meaningful, I think.

My other friend agrees. "My daughter will come upstairs and hand me a piece of paper and say, 'Mommy, I made this just for you!' And I'm like, 'That's so great! That's so nice of you!' The minute she turns her back, it is in the recycling bin."

I did keep the one piece of art where my daughter first colored without going out of the lines. I felt that one was a big deal. But who knows how long I'll keep that? (In fact, I do know that I didn't throw it in the trash, but I have no clue where it is.)

You start to ask yourself, "What are the chances, anyway, that one day my daughter will ask, 'What ever happened to that drawing of the turkey I made for you?'"

The thing is, there's probably a chance. Kids remember the weirdest things.

I live in fear that Rowan will ask me, two days after giving me a drawing she made, "Where is my picture that I colored of the turkey?"

And I probably won't even remember the picture of the turkey—because, let's face it, you can *tell me* you colored a *turkey*, but it looks more like three lines on a page. And, anyway, it's definitely in the garbage, and well on its way to being recycled into probably more paper for future 3-year-old "artistes."

The worst of it, though, is that toddlers expect you to know that three lines on a page is a turkey or a monster or a candy land.

I love it, but hate it, when my toddler shows me her "art" and says, "Guess what I made?"

Now, a toddler asking you what she just made is the equivalent of someone asking if they can try to guess your age, after you turn 30. There's only a fifty percent chance that you'll be happy with the answer. Which are way better odds than actually guessing correctly what your toddler has scribbled. Chances are, your answer is going to be wrong.

"Did you draw a sun?" I'll ask her with trepidation.

"No," she says. "Guess!"

Crap.

"Is it the moon?" I ask, praying to god that's what she drew on the paper that she is holding in front of my face.

"No. I didn't draw the moon," she'll say. Even though it's a scribble that sort of looks like a circle.

"Did you draw Disneyland?" I'll ask.

"Yes! That's what I drew!" she'll say happily. (Though she's never been.)

"I knew it!" I'll say.

The best way to answer the toddler question, "Guess what I made, Mommy?" is with a, "You tell me!"

That puts the onus back on them. I learned this trick the hard way, after making too many wrong guesses about one pink line Rowan drew across a white piece of paper. I was, apparently, a moron for not *knowing* it was a kangaroo.

And then there's the artwork you definitely can't throw out. These are the pieces of art that were actually very important pieces of information before your toddler found them and had decided to scribble all over them. Things like the contacts of all the parents in your toddler's pre-school or the bills you need to pay.

Still, every time I open the trash, I can't help but wonder if I'm making a huge mistake. What if, on that one percent chance, she actually does turn into the next Monet? And then when they interview me, the mother of this artist, I'll have to admit that I saw no genius, saved nothing she made in her early years—*that I threw it all into the trash can?* I'll be the idiot mother who didn't see a future genius in the making. And then I'll never be able to make any money from eBay.

And that would be unfortunate. So maybe I will save at least a couple of those pompoms stuck on a paper napkin with glitter glue in a safe place.

You just never know.

The Banana Phone

Toddlers may as well be talking into a banana, because they sure don't understand the concept of a real phone conversation.

Just because your toddler knows what a phone is and can say "phone" and loves to play with your cellphone does not make them a phone person. Getting a toddler to talk on a phone is painful. Listening to them trying to talk on a phone is even more painful.

First of all, you have to bone them up for the event.

"Let's call grandma and grandpa!" I'll say, like we've just won $6 million in the lottery.

Most of the time, while she's on the phone, I'll be whispering, "Talk into the mouthpiece. *Into the mouthpiece!*"

Then I'll have to crouch by the phone alongside her, trying to hear what Grandma or Grandpa is asking so I can whisper the answer into her other ear. It's all too much. The worst is when she's in a bad mood and doesn't want to speak.

"No. No," she'll scream, pushing the phone away.

And I'll be, like, "Tell them what you did today," to which my toddler will say, "Grass."

As if Grandma and Grandpa are supposed to understand that along with grass we went to the park.

The best is that she doesn't quite understand that people can't see through the phone. She'll point to things in our house while she's talking on the phone, fully expecting other people to know what she's pointing at. Poor Grandma and Grandpa have no idea.

Sometimes, she'll actually have a picture book in her lap and start saying, "Ladybug, cloud," but Grandma and Grandpa have no idea that she has a picture book in her lap and is looking at pictures.

The point is, you think having a conversation with a toddler is hard. But having a phone conversation is even harder.

Once a week, my daughter sleeps at my parents' house. I'll always want to talk to her on the phone.

I'll be in the middle of asking her what she's doing and she'll suddenly say, "Okay, BYE!" It hurts. It does. Which is why I'm trying to get her to practice.

Even when she has a real-life person on the other end—i.e., Grandma and Grandpa—sometimes my daughter prefers to speak on her fake phone, the plastic yellow one that is attached to a plastic toy car.

"I'm going to make a phone call," she'll say. And I'll try to explain that we can make a real call. She's not interested.

"Okay, bye!"

I feel even worse when it's her father calling from work.

"Well, that was a great conversation," he'll say after my daughter has said. "Yup. Nope. Okay, BYE!"

And then I'll feel guilty and explain that she's in the middle of doing something, which she is.

And while she's not interested in talking to Grandma or Grandpa, she'll suddenly get very interested when I make a phone call to the pizza delivery guy. "I want to talk on the phone," she'll say.

One day I was chatting to my friend Jasmine when my daughter decided she wanted to talk to Jasmine, too. I handed her the phone, into which she said absolutely nothing. When I took it away and hung up on Jasmine, my daughter had a complete meltdown.

I actually had to call Jasmine back. Luckily, Jasmine is a very good friend, and she talked to my daughter even though my daughter didn't say a word back.

No matter what happens, you can't win. Whenever I put my toddler on the phone with the Fiancé, I would whisper what she should say into one ear.

"Say, 'I love you,'" I'd tell her.

"I love you," she'd say.

"Say, 'What else is new?'"

"What else is new?" she'd ask her father, which would give him a giggle.

"Tell him you miss him."

"I miss you, Daddy."

Then I'd get back on the phone and he'd say what a great conversation he just had with her, and I'd feel pleased, like I'd just done a good deed. Why not make him happy? But then, one day, he overheard me saying, "Tell him you love him. Tell him you miss him."

When I got back on the phone, he said, "I heard you telling her what to say to me."

"No, she said it all by herself! I swear!"

And, of course, there was the time she was eating French fries and her daddy called from work. I put her on the phone and she said, "Do you want a French fry, Daddy?" and proceeded to try and shove a French fry into the mouthpiece of the phone.

If you can't explain how to speak into the mouthpiece, how can you explain that you can't shove fries through the phone? Though, I wish you could. That would be fantastic!

Little White Lies

It's okay to lie to toddlers. If they don't listen when you say, "Fifteen hours of television is bad for you," just say the television is "busted." They get that. When it comes to toddlers, honesty is not always the best policy.

I lie to my toddler all the time, which is ironic because one of the first lessons we teach our children is that lying is bad. But lying, really, is not bad. It's just easier.

Take this morning, for example. My toddler was watching television and she wanted Elmo. "Where's Elmo?"

The problem with *Sesame Street* is that sometimes Elmo makes an appearance and sometimes he does not. Every two seconds, my daughter would ask, "Where's Elmo? Where's Elmo?"

How do you explain to a 3-year-old that Elmo may not be on this episode? My toddler is already so confused about technology. Sometimes after watching a DVD, she doesn't quite understand that I can't fast forward a regular television show. I couldn't explain the *Sesame Street* thing, so I had to lie.

"I guess Elmo slept in today," I told her.

"Elmo is still sleeping?" she asked.

"Yup. I guess Elmo slept in today," I repeated.

"Why did Elmo sleep in?" she asked.

"I guess he was tired," I told her.

Which seemed to placate her. Lying may be wrong. But it works.

I can't even venture to guess how many times I've lied about things being "broken" only because I didn't want my toddler to use them.

One day, my daughter was dressed all up, perfectly clean and ready to go to a party. But she wanted to paint before we left. She came up to me with paints and I thought, "Oh, no you're not!"

"We're going out now and you are all clean. You can't paint right now," I told her. That was the truth but she wouldn't listen.

"Paint!" she kept saying over and over again.

So I lied. I told her the paintbrushes were "too tired right now." That seemed to placate her.

Lying is good. It's very, very good. At least if you're the parent of a toddler.

One of my friends thought her son was watching too much television so she unplugged it and said it was broken. It remained "broken" for two weeks. One day she and her husband really wanted to watch something and they plugged it back in and turned it on only to find that it really was broken. That's getting bitten in the ass. That's karma for you. That's god reminding you that lying is bad.

Still, here is a list of lies I've told my toddler.

1) The bath has to go to sleep now.
2) The radio is broken.
3) The markers are broken.
4) The balls are broken.
5) The glue has gone to a friend's house.
6) The cupcake was stolen by a mean cupcake fairy.
7) The ice cream man only makes ice cream during the day.
8) Your stuffed animal asked me if she could stay at home and wait for us.
9) My yoga mat says it hurts when you jump on her.
10) Yes, we're in Sweden! (See "Will Maddy Be Wearing Rain Boots?")

Yes, I occasionally—okay, constantly—lie to my toddler. Does that make me a bad mother? I don't think so. And if it does, I can live with it. Because it's easier than the alternative.

Part VI

It's Not Just My Toddler . . . Or Is It?

Mom: How was your day today?

Alexis: Not so good, I got in trouble.

Mom: For what?

Alexis: I told Christina that I talk to god and god told me that he doesn't like her Grandma and she started to cry.

Alexis, 3, daughter of Melissa Huelsman

Toddlers Gone Wild

Your child has taken over your social calendar, your household and every minute of your life. You start missing the days when she was contained in a car seat, couldn't walk and couldn't speak. No one ever told you it got harder as they got older—that the only thing worse than a screaming baby who can't do anything herself is a toddler gone wild.

I'm lucky. I had a few friends who gave birth around the same time I did.

For the first two years of being new parents, we'd try to have civilized meals as a group at least once a week, either at one of their homes or at ours. And by civilized, I mean that we'd hope our babies wouldn't cry nonstop or run into countertops. We'd all split by 7:30 pm.

My friends and I were all waiting anxiously—as we spooned baby food into our babies' mouths and watched that they didn't crawl into the fireplace—for the day when our children could play on their own, without our constant parental supervision.

We waited and waited and waited. The day never seemed to come.

Until, finally, it did.

It happened, one night, when we were all eating takeout Chinese food at my friend's house. We realized that something amazing was happening. We were actually having a—gasp!—conversation, one that didn't include, "Stop that!" "Wipe it up!" or "Share!"

We all shut up and listened to our 2-year-olds playing upstairs.

We continued eating, saying to each other, "This is amazing! They're playing together! They're not hanging off us! Pass the beef and broccoli."

As long as there was no wailing, we figured, all was good.

Except all was not good. Definitely not good.

First came the point when I said, "Um, I haven't heard anything upstairs. They're not making a sound! Should we go check and see if they're alive?" (You can't win being a mother of a toddler. They're either too loud or too quiet.)

Then, another one of us said, "Oh, I'm sure they're fine." So we continued chatting and eating and sipping our wine. But the doubt was in our heads, or at least mine. I'd started to think that maybe our toddlers were being too silent. *Maybe they were up to something.*

I shared my fear with the others, and we headed upstairs. We found our toddlers in the bathroom . . . with the sink tap turned on . . . washing oranges . . . with hand soap.

This is weird in itself—that toddlers think washing oranges is fun—but really, it wouldn't have been an issue if they hadn't used the entire bottle of soap, and if the bubbles hadn't overflowed onto the floor, It wouldn't have been a big deal if my friend's bathroom hadn't been basically flooded and our toddlers as wet as if they had just jumped fully clothed into a pool. Let's just say we were lucky to get there when we did.

Whoever thought there would come a day when you had to explain to your toddler that she just *couldn't wash oranges in the bathroom?*

Who knew where, or when, our toddlers even found the oranges?

What was their thought process—"Hey, let's wash oranges in the sink"?

You can never figure out a toddler's thought process.

This is how toddlers think (at least I think this is how they think):

"Knock, knock," one will say.

"Who's there?" the other will ask.

"Banana!" the first toddler will answer.

"Banana who?" the other will ask.

"Banana light!" the first will answer.

And they'll laugh like it's the funniest thing in the world.

So, of course washing oranges with soap in the bathroom sink seemed like fun.

Another evening, at another friend's house, the grown-ups were all eating in the kitchen while the toddlers played upstairs. "It's so good that they can entertain themselves!" we all said gleefully to one another. "Pass the salad."

This went on for a while, until we noticed that we weren't hearing anything—until we started to ask ourselves, "I wonder if our kids are alive upstairs. I wonder if they're up to something."

I knew that silence was not golden. Silence meant trouble. I plopped down my plate of pasta and ran upstairs. And what did I find? No, our kids weren't washing oranges, but they were all naked and ready to take a bath.

And, they had managed to pour all the bubble bath into the bathtub. We were just lucky that the three 2- and 3-year-old brains couldn't figure out how to turn on the tap.

I had mixed feelings about all of this. On the one hand, I was sort of annoyed. I had no idea my child knew how to undress herself. "If you can undress yourself to get ready to take a bath at someone else's house," I thought, "why do you insist on me undressing you every night?"

On the other hand, I was relieved. If we hadn't raced upstairs when we did, who knows what could have happened.

Then, a few weeks later, the worst thing happened. When I

tell you what happened, you'll think I'm a bad mother. But I'm not a bad mother—toddlers can just be bad.

You put together two toddlers who think that washing oranges is a good idea, and you realize that they feed off each other. They come up with ridiculously stupid ideas, even more ridiculous than washing oranges in a sink or deciding to take a bubble bath together.

Here's what happened. We'd invited a couple over for dinner, the parents of the little boy who is my daughter's best friend. We ordered pizza and all sat down—kids included—to eat. The kids finished in about 2.5 seconds and wanted to go outside to the backyard to play.

The backyard is completely gated.

We left the back door in the kitchen open so they could come in and out, while we continued to eat in the dining room. So there we were, again, saying how wonderful it was that we could eat in peace while our kids played.

Which is ridiculous. By now we should have known that if you leave two toddlers together, without parental supervision, you may get peace, but it always ends badly. I walked into the kitchen to get my friend a beer, only to see piles upon piles of soil on our kitchen floor.

Our toddlers thought it would be a great idea to dig all the soil out of our potted planters and dump it inside our kitchen.

The first lecture began. "YOU DO NOT BRING DIRT INSIDE THE HOUSE!" I screamed at my daughter.

"YOU DO NOT BRING DIRT INSIDE THE HOUSE!" my friend screamed at her son. We brought out the vacuum cleaner and cleaned up the mess while shooing the kids outside.

But while we were cleaning up the soil in our kitchen, I realized, again, that there was total silence from the backyard. I screamed out my daughter's name. My friend screamed out her son's name. We didn't hear anything. I felt a wave of panic like never before.

It was worse than the time in the first month of her life when I rushed her to the emergency room because she had a cold. Where were they? I ran to the front of the house to see the front gate open. My friend ran out with me. We were both screaming their names.

But there's no way they could open the front gate, I thought to myself as I ran and screamed. The lock is way too high for a toddler to reach! The pizza deliveryman must have forgotten to lock it behind him.

I ran out onto the street with my friend in tow, still screaming my daughter's name. And there, halfway down the street on the sidewalk—holding hands, in their bare feet—were our kids.

"GET BACK HERE RIGHT NOW!" I screamed.

My daughter and her best friend looked at each other and laughed.

"GET BACK HERE NOW!" my friend screamed.

Finally, they walked back, still holding hands.

I screamed at my toddler like I'd never screamed at her before, and (of course!) she started to cry. But I was screaming because I cared. She could have been killed or kidnapped or . . . when did they take off their socks and shoes, anyway?

Yes, it's great when toddlers can amuse themselves—as long as it doesn't involve oranges, bubble bath, soil or open gates. While I'm happy they can play with each other, I sometimes miss the day when my toddler was contained in a car seat and couldn't move.

Yes, this is the wonderful world of Toddlers Gone Wild. Buckle your seatbelts. It's a rocky ride.

The Memory Game

Your toddler cannot remember to flush the toilet or put the caps on the markers she just used. But she will remember a promise you made four months ago or that time another kid hit her—last year. Can you say "selective memory?"

My toddler remembers the strangest things. She can't, to save the life of My Pretty Pony or Barbie, remember to flush the toilet, put her shoes on the right feet or put the straw in her mouth *before* she squeezes the apple juice box. But . . .

"Mommy," she said to me this morning, "remember when I was on the yellow slide and I scratched my arm and it hurt? I need a Band-Aid. Remember?"

"Um, you mean when you fell off the yellow slide ten months ago?" I asked in disbelief.

"Yes. I hurt myself on the yellow slide and it hurts. I need a Band-Aid, because I hurt myself on the yellow slide," she said.

"But that was almost a year ago!" I told her.

"But I want a Band-Aid. I hurt myself on the yellow slide!" she cried.

What can I say? The kid has no short-term memory, but an extremely admirable long-term one.

I love how my toddler always forgets the number nine when she counts to ten. I love how she forgets August and November when she goes through the months.

I especially love when she says things like, "Remember when you forgot and gave me the big-person's toothpaste instead of the baby toothpaste and I cried?"

And I'll be, like, "You mean, like, four months ago?"

"Yeah, remember?" she'll ask.

There are advantages to a toddler not having any short-term memory. When I drop my daughter off at school, and she's been a good girl that morning, I'll say, "After school I'll take you to the toy store to buy a little treat."

But then, after a long day at work with no time to eat and a horrendous rush to pick her up, the last thing I'll feel like doing is taking her to the toy store.

Thankfully, because she has no short-term memory, she'll forget about it.

But, oh, she has long-term memory.

Weeks later, having said not a single word about the toy-store promise, she'll scream while she's in the bath, "You said you'd take me to the toy store after school and you never did!"

I suppose, also, that a toddler's memory is like an adult memory. My daughter always remembers the bad things—the scratch from the yellow slide, the time I accidentally (because I was so goddarn tired) put adult toothpaste on her toothbrush, the broken promise—much like I remember more bad things that happen to me than good. The job I never got. The guy who didn't like me back. The pair of sunglasses I lost. I don't remember the jobs I loved, the men who did love me or that I have three other pairs of sunglasses.

"Remember when Evan hit me?" my daughter will ask. "Evan is not nice."

Though she hasn't seen Evan in more than a year, a couple of times a week I'll have to hear about how Evan was mean to her.

My toddler will not only remember things from months ago, but also expect me to know what she's talking about when she remembers these things.

"Remember that MAN? THAT MAN!" she'll demand.

To which I'll be, like, "What man?"

"That man on the street who touched my stroller," she'll say.

Right. Of course I remember. How could I not?

Toddlers also can't let things go.

My daughter will be, like, "Remember when you forgot to bring my stroller and you said you would and you forgot it and you said you would and you forgot my stroller and you said you would and you said you would bring my stroller but you forgot and you said you would?" she'll say.

"Yes, dear, I remember. That was last year."

Or, "Remember when you said I didn't need to bring my umbrella and then it started to rain and I got all wet and you said I didn't need to bring my umbrella and then it rained and I got all wet because you said I didn't need my umbrella, remember?" she'll ask.

"Yes, dear, I remember. That was five months ago," I'll say.

"But do you remember?" she'll ask.

The other day I was getting ready to go out and while I was getting ready, my forgetful-not daughter decided to organize my boots in my closet.

I was obsessed about wearing these new boots I had but when I went to look for them, I couldn't find one.

"Where did you put it?" I asked her. "It was right here!"

"I cleaned up so they're all nice," she told me.

"I know. You just did that. Now where is my boot? You just had it!" I'll scream.

Twenty minutes later, the boot is still nowhere to be found.

"Are you telling me you can't remember where you put my boot you just had two minutes ago?" I'll sigh.

"I put it somewhere so it would be safe," she'll tell me.

"That's great. Where?" I'll ask.

"I don't know. Don't be mad at me," she'll say.

Crap. You can't get mad at your daughter once she looks up at you with her big brown eyes and says, "Don't be mad at me."

Fuck.

Two days later the boot was found in a grocery bag with my old cosmetics under the bathroom sink. I was thrilled!

"Look! I found the boot in this bag with my old makeup," I screamed in delight.

"Mommy, remember you said I could wear makeup when I was a big girl? You said that! Remember? I'm a big girl now. You said I could. You said it! Remember?"

The Car Catnap

This usually occurs two minutes from home, or on the way to do long-overdue chores—the exact moment when you do not want your toddler, who never naps, to fall asleep.

As parents, we spend most of our time trying to get our children to sleep. When Rowan was a baby, spending most of her time awake and wailing, I spent eighteen hours a day trying to get her to sleep. Even now, I spend what seems like hours of my evening trying to get her to stay put in her bed and fall asleep.

It's kind of weird, looking back, to realize how much of my parenting life has been focused on sleep.

As you can probably guess, my daughter was never a napper. Some parents have "nappers" (hate them). I have friends who have children who nap for three to four hours every afternoon. I have friends whose toddlers nap both in the morning *and* the afternoon (really hate them).

But regardless of how important the ability to nap is (and it is important), there comes a time in every parent's life when we do not want our children to go to sleep.

Take the Car Catnap. The Car Catnap is one of the most unfortunate experiences associated with being a parent.

The Car Catnap is what happens when you are driving to or home from somewhere, like the grocery store, or the bank, and you look back and see that your toddler is fast asleep, heading bobbing in her car seat.

"Oh, no," you think to yourself. "Not now! We're two seconds away from our destination. Wake up! Hello? You back there! Wake up! You never nap! Why do you have to fall asleep now? It's almost bedtime!" Or, "We really need groceries! Don't fall asleep now!"

The other night, for example, we were heading home from a quick grocery shop—a car ride that's all of eight minutes long. Just as I was turning onto our street, I noticed that my daughter was fast asleep.

"Hey!" I yelled. "We're almost home!"

I scared the crap out of her, momentarily, like I'd jumped out of a closet and yelled, "BOO!"

And I felt bad about that. But she just looked at me, glassy-eyed, and then her eyes shut again and she was out cold. I pulled into the garage and thought, "This sucks!"

Car Catnaps are problematic for a number of reasons. In this instance, for example, I had a ton of grocery bags to carry into the house. Adding a thirty-pound load (my daughter) just wasn't going to happen.

And here's the other thing about Car Catnaps. You may feel a tinge of relief at the sight of your child sleeping soundly. You may think that all you'll need to do is carefully undo the seatbelt around the car seat, gently pick up your kid, and carry her straight up to her bedroom. Then you'll slowly and quietly change her into her pajamas and nighttime Pull-Ups and put her to bed. In this fantasy, she'll remain asleep for the entire process and then sleep through the night.

This is what I call the "Transfer."

You may also think that if your child falls asleep on the way home on a Saturday afternoon after doing chores, you can just "Transfer" her into her bed, where she will nap peacefully for a couple of hours.

You'd be wrong.

The Transfer from the car to a bed never works. Never.

Your child will not remain asleep once you take her out of her car seat. If you're lucky, you may make it up to her bedroom. You may even lay her down on her bed, thinking, yes, she can sleep in her clothes. But just as you turn to leave the room, she'll wake up. And it blows.

No toddler wakes up from a Car Catnap in a good mood. Ever. Toddlers wake up from Car Catnaps as cranky as I am when I go down to the kitchen after four hours of sleep and realize there's no goddamn coffee left. They wake up cranky and then you're stuck grocery shopping or banking or hanging around the house with a kid who's crying and screaming at the top of her lungs. Either that, or they wake up hyper, usually right before their bedtime.

Car Catnaps are *especially* horrendous if they happen in the afternoon on your way to somewhere you have to be—like a birthday party. Then, for sure, you have to wake them up from the Car Catnap, because you've just dragged your ass halfway across town to attend little Jimmy's third birthday party and you went out and bought the present and everything.

So there you are in your car, trying to wake your child (who, obviously, is tired). "We're here! We're at the birthday party," you'll say, your voice brimming with false enthusiasm. "It will be so much fun, so get up, sleepyhead!" And she won't buy it, not for one minute. She'll just start to cry crankily because you've woken her up from her three-minute nap. If your toddler has a Car Catnap on the way to a birthday party, she won't give a rat's ass if there's going to be cake.

Most parents will do just about anything to avoid the Car Catnap. If the Fiancé is driving and I see that our daughter is about to fall asleep and we're almost home, I'll turn into a freakin' circus act. I'll sing songs (rather, yell them), I'll make funny faces, I'll twist myself around in my seat so I can tickle her or play This Little Piggy. I'll do anything so she doesn't fall asleep in the few minutes it will take for us to pull into the driveway.

The only people, I think, who can really deal with Rowan's Car Catnaps are her grandparents. That's because they have endless patience and never really have to do chores with her. They'll pick her up somewhere and if she falls asleep on the way home, they will literally drive around for two hours until she wakes up on her own. Or they'll buy a paper and park the car somewhere and read it until she wakes up. Who but grandparents has the time and patience to do that?

God, I'm sure, is laughing at me when my toddler takes a Car Catnap.

I can picture him talking down to me: "Rebecca, you prayed to me, wanting your child to sleep more. I have granted you your wish!"

To which I would like to tell god, "Hey, god, I would like to amend my prayer a little. Yes, I'd like her to sleep more, but not in the car minutes away from a birthday party, or right before we get to the grocery store, or right before we're heading home at bedtime. If you could just take care of that, god, I'd really appreciate it. Okay?"

No, But, Why

You will hear these three words coming out of your toddler's mouth over and over again. You will fight the urge to tape her mouth shut.

There are three different stages in a toddler's verbal life. The stages could be called: "Annoying," "more annoying" and "extremely annoying." Or, perhaps, "no," "but" and "why."

The "No" stage started the day my daughter turned two.

"Time for bed," I'd tell her.

"No," she'd respond.

"Get into your pajamas, please," I'd say sweetly.

"No," she'd say, with a smile.

"Get into your pajamas now!" I'd say, not as sweetly.

"No?" she'd say, as if the word were a question.

Or . . .

"Do you want grapes?" I'd ask her after dinner.

"No," she'd say.

"Do you want apples?" I'd ask.

"No," she'd answer. "I want grapes."

"You just said you didn't want grapes. So you want grapes, then?"

"No," she'd say.

"Do you want to stop saying, 'No?'"

"No . . . Apples?"

It's no coincidence that you will enter the "no" stage at the same time as your toddler. You will find yourself saying "No" 264 times a day.

I once wondered how often I said the word "No" to my daughter throughout the day. I decided to do an experiment. I'd make a check on a piece of paper every time I said the word.

I stopped after twenty-one checks because they all happened within twelve minutes.

"Play with paint on walls?" she'd ask.

"No!" I'd say.

"Jump on couch?" she'd ask.

"No!"

"Put potato chips on floor?"

"No!"

"Eat Vaseline?"

"No!"

"Climb on roof and jump off?"

"NO!"

Then comes the "But . . . but . . . but" stage. Since the transition from one stage to the next is gradual, you'll still be saying a hell of a lot of "No's," while your toddler will have moved on to saying "but" all the time.

"Play with paint on walls?"

"No!" you'll say.

"But . . . but . . . but . . . I like paint," your toddler will say.

"NO!" you'll say.

"Put potato chips on floor?"

"No!"

"But . . . but . . . but . . . the floor is hungry!"

"No, the floor is not hungry!"

"Can I—"

"No!" you'll say.

"But . . . but . . . I just want to tell you something," your toddler will say as she gets out of bed for the twelfth time in the last six minutes.

"What is it?" you'll ask, as she comes into the kitchen. (No matter how many times this happens, I still fall for the whole, "But I just have to tell you something . . ." thing.)

"But . . . but . . . but . . . I just want to tell you something. But . . . but . . . I just want to tell you something," she'll say.

"Okay, what?" I'll ask.

"But . . . but . . . I like the sun."

"I like the sun, too. Now go to bed," I'll say.

"But . . . but . . . Mommy . . . but I like the moon," she'll say.

"I like the moon, too," I'll say. "Now get to bed. I'm serious!"

"But . . . I . . . but . . . I like . . . but I like leaves! But!"

And so it goes. No matter what they say to you, the sentence will begin with "but," have a "but" in the middle and sometimes finish with a "but" as well.

"But I don't want to go to bed, but I'm hungry, but I don't like chocolate ice cream, but I'm not 6 yet, but Evan hit me, but I'm not his friend, but I want to watch television, but I like red, but water is wet, but I don't like that pillow, but spiders are scary," is a typical sentence.

And then—just as you're getting used to the "buts"—you'll find yourself in the "Why?" stage, which is by far the most annoying stage and seems to last the longest (we're still in the midst of it and it's been months).*

It's also the stage that will make you feel the dumbest, like maybe you should go back to Grade 2 . . . and 3 . . . and 4. Like you're definitely not smarter than a fifth grader.

"Why is it raining?" my toddler will ask. "Why does it rain?"

It's a good question. Why the hell does it rain? And why the hell don't I know?

"Because the clouds are sad? They're crying," I'll say, thinking I should have paid way more attention in science class (is that where one would learn why it rains?).

"Why are the clouds sad? Why are they crying?" she'll then ask.

"I don't know," I'll tell her.

"But why are the clouds sad?" she'll ask again.

"I don't know."

"But why are the clouds sad?" she'll ask for the third time.

Or . . .

"Why is that man wearing a coat?" she'll say while we're out for a walk. And I'll feel all happy and warm inside because I can actually answer this question.

"Because it's cold outside," I'll answer confidently.

"Why is it cold outside?" she'll ask.

"Because it's fall. Summer is hot and then in fall it gets chilly," I say, feeling my confidence lowering.

"Why is it fall?" she'll ask.

"Because after summer comes fall."

"But why does fall come after summer?" she'll press.

At which point I kind of want to pull out my hair. But I also start thinking, "Why *does* fall come after summer? Who thought of that?"

"Just because," is not a good answer. I've tried the "just because."

"Just because," I'll say when she asks something like, "Why are those flowers red?"

"Why are they red?"

"Just because," I'll say.

"Just because why?"

"What?"

"Why what?" she'll say.

And so it goes.

And then there are the even more difficult questions—questions that have nothing to do with science, geography and math. These questions will make you ask yourself, "How did I grow to be a productive member of society? Seriously. How?"

"Why is my birthday October 15?" she'll ask.

"Because that's the day you were born," I tell her.

"Why?" she'll ask.

"Because it is. You were born on that day. That's your birthday," I'll tell her.

"No, my birthday is on Halloween," she'll tell me.

"No, it's not!" I'll respond. (See how quickly you revert back to the "no" stage?)

"But . . . but . . . I want my birthday to be on Halloween," she'll whine. And you know that you are on the verge of a meltdown and it's just not worth it.

"Okay, fine. Your birthday is on Halloween," you'll find yourself saying.

I may not know many of the answers to her questions, but I do know this: when your child is asking you something, you have to have some sort of an answer. You must.

Toddlers don't know that not looking up from your paper is code for "stop talking please." They don't know that, "I don't know" means "Can we end this conversation?"

"Why do cars have tires?" my daughter asked me last week.

"So they can drive?" I answered.

"Why do they drive?"

Sigh.

And I know that she's only going to make me feel stupider the older she gets. Because she'll get homework—actual homework—and then I'll be really fucked.

One of my friends admitted to me that her son came home from school recently with a map of Canada to fill out. She had to ask her husband to help point out all the provinces.

I know this makes her sound stupid, but I completely get it. You become stupider as a parent. There's the whole sleep deprivation thing, and the loss of brain cells (I swear, they die off during the birthing process) and television. Maybe television *does* make you stupider, but you don't really care. You'll still be in front of it most nights.

"Why are there rainbows?" my toddler asked me just the other day.

What exactly is a mother supposed to do when she doesn't know the answer? I finally figured it out. When a mother has absolutely no idea why there are rainbows, she "uses her imagination!" She makes things up. In other words, she lies.

"So the fairies can slide down them for fun!" I told my daughter. Why not? Doesn't Barney teach us to use our imaginations?

"Why do they slide down rainbows for fun?" she asked.

"Um, because it's fun?" I said.

"But why?"

Which leaves me to ask, "Why, oh why, oh why do they ask so many questions?" I kind of miss the "no!" stage.

* Please note that less than three weeks after writing this essay I learned there is an even more annoying stage than "Why." This is the "copying" stage, in which I say something like, "Stop jumping on the bed and get your socks on," and my toddler responds with, "Stop jumping on the bed and get your socks on," to which I respond, "Now!" to which she responds, "Now!" to which I look up to god and respond, "What did I do to deserve this?" to which she says, "What did I do to deserve this?"**

** Please note that after writing the above paragraph we also entered the "Watch this!" stage. "Watch this, Mommy! Watch this! Watch this! Watch this!"***

*** Please note that the stages never end.

The Very Public Meltdown

This temper tantrum occurs when there are many, many other witnesses—people who are judging you and wondering, "Why don't you have any control over your child? What kind of parent are you?"

How wrong is it, exactly, to pretend your child is not yours?

Isn't it like if you fart in a room, and you know everyone can smell it, so you look around pointedly at everyone else, pretending it wasn't you, that it must have been someone else? Everyone does that, right?

Well, the other day, as my daughter lay screaming on the floor in an airport, I had the brief inclination to pretend that the screaming *thing* at my feet—the thing flailing her arms and legs—was not mine.

She was *so* not mine. She was *so* someone else's fart.

In fact, I kind of stood there, looking down at her and wondering if anyone would believe that she wasn't mine. Unfortunately, she really does look like me. But at that moment, I didn't want her to be mine. I wanted to crawl into a ball, put my hand over my ears, and sing, "La la la, I can't hear you!" I wanted to click my heels and be . . . anywhere else but there.

There's nothing like the Very Public Meltdown, also known as the Very Public Temper Tantrum, otherwise known as the Thing You Fear the Most. For some parents, it happens every day. Luckily it doesn't happen all that often for me.

So, when my toddler does have a Very Public Meltdown, I find myself on the verge of a panic attack. It's like when I look at a very complicated math equation. I have no idea what to do. (Except to cry, and that wouldn't help the situation.) I want to throw my hands up, throw my pencil down and say, "Forget it! I don't know the answer! I quit!"

Unfortunately, you can't quit your kid.

As a mother, I know how judgmental other mothers can be. But, let's face it: sometimes you can't help but be judgmental, no matter how many times you tell yourself you will *never* be that type of mother.

I've dropped the pacifier and put it back into my toddler's mouth. So why am I looking at that mother doing the same thing and thinking, "That's just wrong!" I will admit, also, that when I see a toddler having a Very Public Meltdown in a playground, I think to myself, "Why is that kid acting that way? Why can't the mother control her offspring?" And then I feel bad for thinking those thoughts, *for being a judgmental mother*, and I start empathizing with the mother instead.

I know now that the Very Public Meltdown usually has nothing at all to do with the mother and everything to do with the toddler. (Can you say, "She gets that from her *father's* side?") But even though I absolutely know this, I still can't help but think, "Why doesn't the mother do something?"

Which, I'm sure, is what every other person was thinking about me while my daughter lay on the airport floor wailing and kicking her legs into the air.

The thing is, I really *didn't* know what to do. If we'd been in a grocery store, I would have just picked her up and left. But we had a plane to catch.

So what led to this Very Public Meltdown? What horror had occurred to send my daughter over the edge? I had handed Rowan one of those little cards you attach to your luggage. You know, the ones that have a space for your name and address in case the airline loses your bags.

In my stupidity, I had given her one because it distracted her while I was checking in. She liked holding the tag.

Until she lost it. The tag, I mean. And then she really lost it, if you know what I mean.

She dropped the luggage tag somewhere between gates 48 and 52, which led to the Very Public Meltdown, just outside gate 53.

"I want the card! I want the card! Where is my card! AHHH-HHHHH!" she screamed.

I looked for the tag on the ground. I couldn't find it. I tried to give her another one. And although this kid ain't that smart—she lost it over a lost luggage tag, after all—she was smart enough to know that the luggage tag I tried to trick her with wasn't the one she'd lost.

In a toddler's mind, if she collapses into a ball on the floor and starts screaming and pounding her fists and kicking her feet, somehow the luggage tag will magically appear again. Of course, it doesn't. And the Very Public Meltdown continues. Very publicly.

I can deal with a temper tantrum at home. Usually it passes after I leave her lying on the floor until she lets it all out. Or I pick her up, lay her on top of me, and rub her back until she calms down.

But the Very Public Meltdown is hard to deal with because, well, you're in *public*. During a Very Public Meltdown, everyone is watching to see how you deal with it, which creates extra pressure to deal with it *as soon as possible, if not sooner.*

You just know that strangers are wondering what the hell kind of parent you are. They're wondering what you did to result in your kid lying and screaming on the floor in an airport. (And since we were in the airport, people were also probably praying that we weren't on the same plane as them.)

But what was I supposed to do? First of all, who knew a kid would get so upset over a lost luggage tag? I certainly didn't, until it happened. It's not like there's a manual out there called, "What to Do When Your Child Screams Bloody Murder When She Loses a Luggage Tag at an Airport."

Second, I couldn't just lie on the airport floor, rubbing her back until she calmed down. People would have thought I was crazy (although I did contemplate it).

So, I did the best I could under the circumstances—the circumstances being that we were late and had a plane to catch and I was carrying a thousand-pound diaper bag, along with my own carry-on.

I just picked her up and started walking. I walked and walked and walked away from all those judgmental eyes (and perhaps a couple of pitying ones), as far from Gate 53 (and the sheer embarrassment of my toddler's meltdown to beat out all other public meltdowns) as I could get.

Eventually she did calm down. The only good thing about temper tantrums is that they do end. Eventually.

Often, in public, I live in sheer fear that my daughter will have a meltdown.

I feel like I'm constantly holding my breath praying, "Okay, not here. Not here."

I don't dilly-dally anywhere anymore. I'm in and out. There's no *browsing* anymore. All because I fear that my toddler will have a tantrum. You just never know.

And that's the thing with toddlers. One second they're happy and fine and laughing and the next second they've lost their luggage tag and they're having a meltdown, screaming bloody murder. And you're convinced if they don't stop screaming someone is going to call social services on you.

And while you may want to pretend your child is someone else's, you can't. She's yours and you're stuck with her—through the good times and the Very Public Meltdowns—until death do you part.

Flight Risk

The only thing passengers hate more than sitting beside a newborn is sitting near a toddler. Oh, the trials of toddler travel.

I no longer feel any sympathy for the passenger sitting next to my toddler on an airplane.

When she was a baby, I *used* to feel sympathy for this passenger. There was a great chance, after all, that my daughter would scream or, worse, puke.

But when my baby morphed into a toddler, I started to feel for the person sitting in the seat *in front* of us. Toddlers don't understand, "Stop kicking the person in front of you." They just don't.

Or they may understand, but since their memories last as long as that of a fruit fly (at least usually—see "The Memory Game"), they forget a split second later. So you spend the entire flight saying, "Stop kicking the chair in front of you! Stop kicking the chair in front of you! Stop kicking the chair in front of you!" like a broken record. In fact, I don't even have to look up from my magazine anymore. I just flip the page and say, "Stop kicking the chair in front of you." By the time I'm finished reading that page, I'll have to say it again.

Once your baby turns into a toddler people expect that she should be old enough to behave. It's like no one on a plane has ever heard the phrase "Terrible Twos" or "Torturous Threes."

It's actually easier to travel with a baby. Passengers, although they may huff and roll their eyes upon finding themselves sitting next to you and your baby, are intelligent enough to know that it's just a baby, for god's sake. People *know* that babies cry and shit and sometimes both. They also know you can't train a baby not to cry.

My poor friend Kama was on a four-hour flight recently and her baby literally cried from the time the plane took off until they reached their destination. By the time the plane landed, Kama was crying too.

But people get that crying babies are frustrating and no fun. Sometimes passengers even look at you with sympathy. Which is nice.

They are less sympathetic about toddlers.

Passengers don't seem to get why your toddler keeps kicking the back of their seat. They don't get why your toddler isn't listening when you telling her not to kick the back of the seat. In fact, the only thing more annoying than being kicked in the back every two seconds may be hearing a mother say, "Stop kicking the chair," every two seconds.

I've come to think that having sympathy for the passengers sitting near your toddler on a plane is a complete waste of energy. Thems the breaks, I now figure.

Yes, it's unfortunate for you that you got the seat in front of a toddler. Yes, it pretty much sucks. But, these days, plane rides aren't fun anyway. You were looking forward to a relaxing flight? Who are you kidding, buster? The food, if you get any, sucks. The plane will probably be delayed. Your seat is likely broken and won't recline. You just saw the movie last week. Face it: a relaxing flight wasn't going to happen anyway.

And, sure, having a toddler sitting behind you adds much more suckiness to your already far-from-relaxing journey, but as I said, thems the breaks. I can't spend my energy worrying about you. I have to spend it trying to shove overfull carry-on bags under the seat, and praying that my toddler doesn't have to pee after the six-foot-tall man in the aisle seat beside us has fallen asleep. And that's all I'm going to worry about.

In the past, whenever someone wasn't nice to me, or I didn't get something I really wanted and had tried hard for, the Fiancé would always say, "Life isn't fair. Get used to it."

That's how I feel about traveling with a toddler. You got seat 17B, and my toddler is in 18B, and that 100 percent falls into the "Life isn't fair. Get used to it" category. And it's not all bad, you know—at least not for the parent. Thanks to my toddler, I am now one of those passengers who also falls into the, "People with small children or who need extra assistance can board first" category. (I absolutely adore this category. How long can I stay in it? It's just so much more relaxing to board at your own pace!) Since I'm already seated when the rest of the passengers board, I get to witness the looks of disappointment as people realize they're sitting next to or in front of a toddler. It's the same look as when they see they're sitting beside a baby.

In fact—and this is evil of me—I get a small jolt of pleasure out of seeing other passengers' looks of utter disappointment. It's just that sometimes the look of horror is so crystal clear on their faces that I can't help but smile inside (and occasionally let out a small giggle).

It's come to this because some people are just downright rude about the whole thing.

On a recent trip with my toddler, things started out well enough. She was sitting silently in her seat, playing with stickers on her pulled-down chair table. This was the scene when a woman sat down in the same row, but across the aisle.

The first thing out of this woman's mouth was, "Are you going to drug her?"

I kid you not.

Now, I *was* planning on drugging my toddler. She had a horrible cold and I was worried about her ears.

Okay, my toddler didn't have a cold, but I was worried about her ears.

Okay, I really wasn't worried about her ears at all.

But Tylenol for Babies does seem to make her drowsy and it was a four-hour flight. Even though I'm her mother and love her to death, I didn't really want to be traveling with a toddler either. (You think sitting on a plane near a toddler is bad? Being a mother and having to be responsible for that toddler on a plane is worse. Have some sympathy for me!)

Anyways, thoughts raced through my head as I tried to figure out how to answer this woman's question.

Thoughts like, "It is *my* toddler, missy, so don't be asking me if I'm going to be drugging her with such *hope* in your voice."

And, "if you *are* going to ask me if I'm planning to drug my child, could you at least say, 'Hi. How are you today?' first? And why are you talking to me anyway? Why don't you just roll your eyes like most people do when they see they're sitting near a toddler?"

I looked at this woman, who had asked me if I was going to drug my child, with a blank stare. I thought about pretending I didn't understand English. Why should I tell her anything, I wondered.

"Maybe," I answered.

(Okay, I had already drugged my child. It's a science, this whole drugging your child before your plane takes off thing. You have to get them drugged at the exact right moment, so they're already drowsy by the time the plane has boarded. You should *never* drug them before you board the plane. I once gave my daughter Tylenol before we got on the plane and then, of course, the plane was delayed for more than an hour, which meant I had a very sleepy/cranky child to carry aboard along with our two carry-ons. And, of course, she woke up twenty minutes into the four-hour flight. Far from fun, I tell you, far from fun.)

But "Maybe" didn't do the trick.

This toddler-drug-pushing passenger then asked me, "Did you bring a lot of toys for her to play with?"

Now I was getting really annoyed. Who *was* this woman to so boldly ask me if I was going to drug my child while simultaneously having the nerve to assume that I was an idiot mother who wouldn't *think* of bringing toys on a four-hour plane ride? What kind of moron mother did she think I was? What kind of mother takes a 3-year-old on a plane with absolutely *nothing* to do?

"Not really," I answered, giving her a blank stare. (*Of course* I brought things for her to do! But I didn't have to answer to this nervy toddler drug-toy-pusher-stranger.)

"I just brought a DVD player for her," I told this woman. Then added, "She's a really good traveler. She just watches and then usually falls asleep."

I hated myself for feeling the need to explain that my toddler was pretty good on airplanes. Especially since I couldn't actually guarantee that my child would be a "really good traveler."

Also, I'm a firm believe in not jinxing things. By saying aloud that my toddler was "usually a really good traveler," I was just asking for her to be as good as a college frat boy during rush week.

"Well, my father used to give me half an Ativan before we traveled when I was a child," this woman told me. "And he was a doctor."

Doh! Did she really expect me to give my 3-year-old half an Ativan? (Especially since if I had any Ativan, I wouldn't be wasting it on my toddler. I'd be taking it myself.)

Flight attendants are sometimes no better when it comes to dealing with toddlers. Once, a flight attendant told me that the other passengers wouldn't like it if the sound on our portable DVD players was on.

Now, portable DVD players can barely be heard, and especially not over the sound of a plane's engine. And, yes, kids shows are super-annoying. But I wanted to ask this flight attendant if the other passengers would rather hear the voice of Elmo or the sound of my child screaming.

There have been times, too, when my toddler and I have not had seats next to one another. These are fun times. I'll walk up to the gate and the grumpy airline worker will say, "I'll see what I can do. But I can't guarantee anything," to which I get to reply, "Well, *I* don't mind if my 2-year-old doesn't sit beside me, but I'm pretty sure the passenger stuck sitting next to her might mind."

And then it will click in. She's only 2! Of course she needs to sit beside her mother.

Then there was the time a border inspector interrogated my 2-year-old.

"What's your name?" he asked my frightened daughter.

She look petrified and said, "Rowan," so softly.

"Where are you going?" he asked.

"Plane."

I wanted to smack this border inspector for terrifying my daughter. But I couldn't. I needed to get through. We had a plane to catch and travelers to torment.

God Bless This Mess!

Is there any point—ever—in organizing your house when you live with a toddler? Even though it was spotless, your house is a complete disaster three seconds after your child gets home. It's a toddler tornado.

Forget about a personal assistant, trainer, masseuse or chef.

What I want, more than anything—including a husband—is a full-time, personal housekeeper.

And I don't mean a housekeeper who just works 9 to 5 once a week.

I need a housekeeper who literally follows me around like a shadow.

Rather, I need a housekeeper who literally follows *my toddler* around like a shadow.

I don't know how it happens. All I know is that if my toddler is in the house for any length of time longer than thirteen seconds, my home turns into something I imagine a daycare would look like if they let all twenty-five children run around freely for three hours.

I swear, even if my toddler has slept for the entire night and just gotten out of bed, somehow the house seems as if either a tornado has swept through it or I've been burglarized.

Some days, I actually find myself looking around wondering, "Wait . . . maybe someone did break in . . . Did they?"

When I worked full-time and my daughter was 2, we had a full-time nanny. I would come home from my office and the house would be clean as a whistle. The nanny would leave and, by the time the Fiancé came home from work, the house would be a complete disaster.

I really don't know how it happened. I always blamed myself for just being plain bad at housework (and so did the Fiancé), but now I know it's not me. It's the toddler.

My toddler and I have a morning routine. We wake up, I carry her into the kitchen, plop her into her highchair, and turn on the television. So far, no mess. I make her frozen microwavable pancakes, she eats them and then I get her dressed for pre-school. No problem, right?

By the time I'm running out the door, the house—which I swear I spent an hour organizing last night before I went to bed—is completely turned upside down.

How does this happen? We've been out of bed for only an hour! But there are her pajamas in a ball on the floor. Her dirty plate on her highchair. An apple juice box on the counter. All her stuffies—what she calls stuffed animals—on the floor. Her shoes in a messy pile by the door (she's rifled through them to find the pair she wanted to wear). Her hair clips on the kitchen floor. And on and on.

Sometimes, my single, child-free friends will ask how it is being a mother. I tell them that along with being a mother, I feel like a full-time housekeeper. I always find myself cleaning up something, picking up crayons, wiping something sticky off something else.

It's never-fucking-ending. They should really name hurricanes after toddlers. And forget about *after* school.

She walks in the door. Her uniform is thrown on the floor and she rifles through her drawers to find something to change into. She decides she wants to play memory cards, all fifty pieces of which are then all over the floor. Then she'll want a snack, which means the banana peel—along with pieces of banana—will end up everywhere *but* in her mouth. She'll want to color, and there's no use telling her to take just one marker out at a time. (And why the hell do companies have to come up with the "JUMBO BOX! 350

MARKERS!" How about a box that reads, "Just TWO markers!") Caps and markers and pieces of paper will end up all over the place. And then she'll decide she's bored with that and go into her toy chest, even though she doesn't really want anything from the toy chest. (It's kind of like how adults look into the fridge without actually being hungry.) She'll dump everything out piece by piece, toy by toy, until the entire floor is covered. And then it's 4 o'clock.

Yes, all of this happens in a span of twenty minutes. After which I'll think, "No, seriously. While you were at school I cleaned up everything. I could see my face in the shine of the floor!"

I'm not going to lie to you. I have someone come in every day. And I made things clear to the agency: "I don't want someone so much to look after my child as to clean up," I said. To anyone who is not a parent, this sounds awful. But I don't need someone to look after my daughter. I'm around to do that. I just can't keep up with the mess! It's like the mess travels at the speed of light. In the blink of an eye, my organized home turns into something out of a bad reality television show where the hosts come in and say, "How do you live like this?" and "Let's get you organized!"

Honestly, the Fiancé will sometimes come home and say, "What happened in here? It's a fucking disaster!" And I'll have to remind him that we have a toddler and that this is what happens when you have a toddler.

So, if you want to save your relationship and keep some sort of sanity, hire a full-time housekeeper. It will help. I swear.

Technicolor Toddlers

Your toddler insists on dressing up in a Halloween costume to go out, even though it's June. Even worse, toddlers sometimes want to pick out their own outfits. It's wrong to be embarrassed to be seen out in public with your own child . . . but you kind of are.

I saw Superman this morning.

He came in the form of a little boy, dressed in a Halloween costume.

In my pre-motherhood days, I would not have been sitting in a pancake house at 8 a.m. on a Saturday morning. In my pre-motherhood days, I would not have understood why there was some kid, *in July*, walking the streets wearing a Superman costume before I had even had my coffee.

But I'm the mother of a toddler now. Not only am I at a pancake house at 8 a.m. on a Saturday morning, but I barely bat my eyes as Superman walks by.

Why would I? My toddler is dressed, at present, as a princess. She has a tiara on her head and five plastic bead necklaces around her neck.

Toddlers don't care if it's Halloween or not. Once they get something in their heads, that's it. If your toddler wants to dress as a pumpkin to go out for pancakes, she's going to dress as a pumpkin to go out for pancakes. If she wants to wear a dress-up princess costume, instead of one of the hundreds of real dresses she has in her closet, that's what she's going to wear. It's just not worth the fight, even though the Fiancé is usually all, like, "She's going out like that? Are you serious?"

This morning, after the toddler emerged from her bedroom in full toddler costume, I explained to the Fiancé that it's not that big a deal, really. After all, I told him, we have to pick our battles. Let's save the fight for when she wants to leave the house in a bra and fishnet stockings. Plus, I want some damn pancakes, so let's just go already.

The first time my daughter wanted to wear her princess costume out in public was to a mall. I can't believe I actually tried to talk her out of it. It was a waste of breath. She just didn't get why she couldn't wear her dress-up costume outside the house.

The problem is that people—and by people, I mean those who don't have to have this argument before leaving the house—think it's adorable when a child is out in public in a costume. They'll be, like, "Aw, that's so cute!" They'll coo, "Isn't she adorable?"

Which, you know, toddlers absolutely adore hearing.

The more whacked-out a toddler dresses, the more compliments she receives.

One toddler I know gets very upset when she walks into a store and people don't say how cute she is. "Mommy," she said to her mother recently, after they walked out of a store, "Why didn't that lady tell me how cute I was?"

"It must have slipped her mind," her mother told her.

As parents, we're always telling our kids how adorable they are, twenty times an hour. They come to expect it.

My toddler thinks it's fine—more than fine, in fact; she thinks it's the right thing to do—to wear a costume out in public when it's not a dress-up party or Halloween. She'll just ask, "Don't I look adorable?"

Sometimes, though, costumes are preferable to your toddler's own clothes—especially when they start picking out their own outfits. When your toddler decides that she wants to pick out her own clothes, well, let's just say that it's the end of your child looking . . . sane.

That's because it's the end of "matching."

In a toddler's eyes, a pink and purple polka-dotted shirt *does* match with green and black-striped pants. The outfit, in fact, looks even better with rainbow-colored socks, fake necklaces and red shoes!

"She picked her own outfit!" I always used to say to people when my toddler first started picking out her own clothes. I always felt like I had to justify her pimped-out look. I felt like adding, "No, you don't understand. She has beyond-gorgeous clothes at home! Really. I didn't dress her!" But what was the point?

You'll see other toddlers show up to music class wearing tutus over jeans and tank tops over long-sleeved shirts, and these mothers will say to you, "She picked out the outfit herself," in the same justifying tone you have also used. You just want to say to these discomfited moms, "Really, I get it. No explanation needed."

You just kind of have to get over it.

Toddlers are very proud of the outfits they choose.

"Don't I look beautiful?" my toddler will ask me, twirling in her striped red and orange socks, silver shoes, red velvet dress and a yellow sweater.

All you can do is say, "Yes, you are the most beautiful girl in the whole world!" You can't say to your own flesh and blood, "You look, well, a little C-R-A-Z-Y. I'm kind of embarrassed to be seen with you."

And it's not just clothes. It's accessories. My toddler thinks Band-Aids are accessories. What could I say when she insisted on wearing a red Band-Aid on the middle of her forehead one day? Not only did she look C-R-A-Z-Y but people kept bending down and asking her, "What happened to you?"

And I'd have to cover her ears and say, "Nothing happened. She just wants to wear a Band-Aid across her forehead. I swear!" (I did put my foot down the time she wanted to wear a Band-Aid across her nose. I was not going to spend the whole day explaining that, no, my 3-year-old did not have a nose job—she's just insane!)

I thought the getting-dressed routine would get easier once my toddler could put her clothes on herself. Wrong. It's only getting harder.

Now that she's into choosing her own clothes, she comes up with ideas like, "Today is bow day. Everything I wear must have a bow on it." Which is why, three days ago, she was wearing orange socks with a bow, a pink and gray wrap dress with a bow on the back, and leggings with colorful butterflies that I had convinced her weren't really butterflies but bows. Even her shoes needed to have bows, which meant we went out in public with her wearing hot-pink slippers, because they were the only footwear she owned with bows.

Then there was "flower day," when everything she wore had to have a flower on it. Which is why we left the house, two days ago, with her wearing a red shirt with a flower, pink tights with flowers, blue pants with flowers on the pockets and yellow socks with black flowers.

I could go on. There has also been "rainbow day," "cookie day"—don't ask—and "Elmo day," which was the worst theme day ever. It ended up with me gritting my teeth while trying to explain that we just don't have an Elmo skirt, underwear and pants, and that the only Elmo item of clothing we own is a T-shirt, and begging if we could please, please, please go back to "flower day."

My friend's 3-year-old daughter went to school dressed in the most ridiculous outfit one day. "Nothing matched. Not even her two socks. When I walked into the classroom with her, even the teacher took one look at her and said, 'Oh my god.'"

You know it's bad when a teacher who has been working with toddlers for two decades says, "Oh my god," when she sees what your toddler has put on.

Another friend's toddler insisted on wearing numerous hair clips to her daycare. "I swear to god," this mother tells me, "she had about fifteen clips in her hair. She looked like a Christmas tree. It was ridiculous."

But it all worked out. "She actually started a trend. For the next couple of days all the little girls came to daycare with multiple hair clips," this mother added. (So maybe her toddler is actually fashion forward, the next Mary Kate or Ashley Olsen.)

Boys don't seem to dress as ridiculously as girls. This is possibly because there just aren't as many clothing options and colors for boys (instead of complaining, you should be grateful!). But, apparently, there's still room to experiment.

One of my friends says that while her toddler son usually matches (and not just because of his "all green" outfit—which is almost as ugly as mismatching because he looks like a mini version of the Jolly Green Giant), there are times he demands to wear the same shirt every single day for a month.

"We had to wash this one shirt with a truck on it every night because he refused to get dressed in anything else. That's almost worse than having a girl dressed weirdly, because people thought that my kid was wearing filthy clothes or that we didn't have any other clothes for him except this one shirt," she told me. (It's kind of like being in a gym class and noticing that the person next to you is wearing the exact same workout clothes as yesterday . . . and the day before . . . and the day before that. You *do* wonder if they wash them or not.)

A tiny part of me wonders if this is our fault—if we are to blame for the fact that toddlers don't get the concept of "matching."

There are the days when you're running late and your toddler is jumping naked on the bed and agrees to get dressed only if you let her pick the outfit herself. "Does this match?" she'll ask.

And because you are late, and because you most certainly can't deal with another wardrobe change, you say, "Yes! It matches! Plaid and polka-dots always match!"

Back at the pancake house, Superman's mother walked past the window and saw my princess. We gave each other a little, knowing smile.

It was just another day in Toddler Land.

Part VII
It's Not Just Me . . . Or Is It?

Samuel: Mommy, it's like you and I are on a date!

Mommy: Oh yeah, this is exactly like a date.

Samuel: Because I'm a boy and you are a girl. If I was a girl, we couldn't be on a date. You are so lucky I'm a boy.

Mommy: Actually, two girls can go on a date.

Samuel: But they couldn't kiss.

Mommy: Yes they could, actually. They could even get married!

Samuel: (after a long pause) So two boys can kiss and get married?

Mommy: Sure!

Samuel: (again after a long pause) That's great. I'm going to go out and find me a boy to kiss right now!!

Mommy: (after her own long pause . . . thinking, "What is your grandfather going to say about that?") That's great, Sam!

Samuel Biebrier, 3, son of Daphne Gilbert

A Little Thing Called Appreciation

Your toddler SO does not appreciate everything you do. And this makes you think about how much you should have appreciated your own mother. Appreciation should be one of the "magic" words.

There's a word I've come to really understand since becoming a mommy—along with "Night-Time Pull-Ups," "washable markers" and "childproof."

That word is "appreciation."

I've never felt so unappreciated in my life.

At the same time, I also feel like I am the worst daughter in the world.

I'm not talking about the big bad things I did growing up, things my parents still don't know about. (I still have an irrational fear that I will get grounded for sneaking butts in the furnace room in the basement after my parents left for work. Not that I did that . . . it's just an example . . . really.) I'm talking about the little things that my mother used to do that annoyed *me*—like when she would come home after grocery shopping for a family of six and call for help bringing the bags up.

I'd roll my eyes as if this was the most annoying request ever.

I was such a friggin' brat.

Now that I have my very own brat, I see the world in a whole new light. There's nothing like being a mother to make you realize the importance of appreciation.

Toddlers don't appreciate anything. Of course they don't! They can't *pronounce* the word let alone understand its meaning. (And, hey, who can blame them? I just basically learned the meaning myself.)

But after you've made a trip to the toy store and made your toddler dinner—taking out all the carrots, celery and chicken in the noodle soup by hand (and feeling like a handler of a rock star who demands only red M&M's)—and run a bath, and shampooed and blow-dried her hair, and wiped her ass for what seems like the millionth time, and your toddler says, "You get that for me!" even though what she wants is a stuffed animal and it's *right by her feet*, you can't help but feel really underappreciated.

You actually bite your tongue to stop yourself from saying, "Do you not appreciate anything I've done for you?" because you don't want to end up sounding like your mother.

So, I'd just like to take this opportunity to say, "I'm sorry, Mom. I appreciate you and everything you've done."

Also, do you, by any chance, want to baby-sit tonight?

The Mother's Day Rant

No one can live up to the high expectations you set for only THE most important day of the year. And—surprise, surprise!—it's no longer Valentine's Day. It's Mother's Day.

I haven't done the Valentine's Day Rant in ages. I have, however, done the Mother's Day Rant.

Once you get to celebrate the day, you realize that Mother's Day is even more important than Valentine's Day. The expectations are higher. You don't just hope that, at the very least, your partner has dropped into the flower store on his way home from work. You don't consider yourself lucky if you get a box of chocolate *and* a bouquet.

Things have changed, after all. You are no longer just a girlfriend who is good in bed. You're a mother now. You gave birth to this man's child. You are raising this man's child. You are so much more than a girlfriend, and because you know you are so much more than a girlfriend, your expectations become higher. You deserve flowers, chocolate *and* a handbag or piece of jewelry.

As one of my friends says each and every year, "I was in labor for forty-eight hours! Damn right, I deserve a good Mother's Day!" (This is why you should never brag about "easy" labors. Once you say it was "easy," there's no moaning about why you deserve that Chanel bag.)

There was a point when I thought that no mother in the world ever had a good Mother's Day. That was two years ago, when my daughter was 2, and I wanted to spend the day with her. It was Mother's Day, after all, and although she couldn't buy me a present herself, that didn't mean she didn't want to hang with me.

But there was a "miscommunication." My daughter didn't

come home from the In-laws' house at 1 p.m. like she was supposed to and they weren't answering their cellphone, so I spent most of that Mother's Day ranting at the Fiancé, "Where are they? Where are they?" getting madder and madder as the day went on.

By the time my daughter came home from the park, she was exhausted and cranky, the Fiancé was mad at me and I just had to be . . . her mother. It wasn't special at all! It was like any other day of the year.

That was also the same year three of my friends had horrible Mother's Days, too.

I called one of them the following day and asked her how her day had been.

"Don't ask," was all she said. "I don't want to talk about it."

My other friend's husband actually forgot, which means he's either completely clueless or that my friend should really follow in my footsteps and start reminding him a month before that, "Mother's Day is just around the corner!"

My third friend had a bad day because she had to visit her mother and her husband's mother (whom she doesn't like all that much) so she spent most of her day on the road with her toddler who gets car sick.

Men don't like Mother's Day. I think they actually prefer Valentine's Day. First off, it's easier to show your appreciation for someone you love than to the mother of your child (because that's *big*).

Second, I think that most mothers—like me—believe that they should either get a really big present from their partner and children, or two presents—one from their partner and one from their child. But because toddlers think that "money comes from the money store," they can't very well go out and buy a gift. So it's up to the father to buy *two* gifts.

Now, before you think I'm just a gift whore, I'd like to say that you are right. I am a gift whore. But I also firmly believe that the most important part of the gift is the card.

Men are not good at writing cards because they're not good at sharing their feelings.

I may love the designer bag my partner bought me for Mother's Day, but I'm always a tad disappointed when I see a card with, "Happy Mother's Day" scribbled out. And that's it.

No thought went into that card. On Valentine's Day, you can get away with a simple, "I love you," and the words don't even have to be written out! They can be pre-printed on a card that hangs around the neck of a teddy bear.

"What do you expect?" you're probably thinking. It's a good question. What *do* I expect? How can I expect a guy to write something that will sum up how much he loves the fact that I'm the mother of his child, and everything I do for that child, when I spend most of the time complaining about it?

If you're single in your third decade, you've probably learned to lower your expectations for Valentine's Day. In the same vein, I've come to think that mothers (or at least I) must lower their expectations for Mother's Day. That way, when your partner decides to make breakfast for you with your toddler, and your toddler decides to empty half the bag of flour into the cutlery drawer, and you do get your pancakes but also the mess to clean up after, you won't feel all that let down.

Mothers need to take Mother's Day back into our own hands. We have to stop expecting the fathers of our children to do something.

But even this is tricky.

Because the other issue that makes Mother's Day way more complicated than Valentine's Day is that you are torn between actually wanting to spend the day with your child and wanting to spend the day without your child. A good Valentine's Day, for most people, is one spent with someone. You never debate whether you should spend Valentine's Day with your boyfriend/partner or not. You just do it and try not to brag about it to your single friends.

But as a mother, you don't know which way to go. Would you have more fun at the spa? How can you not be with your own child on Mother's Day?

And what if you are also still a daughter in addition to being a mother? You might be expected to spend the day with *your* mother, which may seem a bit like a chore—and should you really be doing chores on Mother's Day?

Still, we need to be proactive and book that day at the spa, buy our own presents and enjoy it. (One of my friends got upset at her husband on Mother's Day when he just told her to, "Go buy yourself something you want." I told her she really should go out and buy that $1,800 Chanel bag she'd been eyeing. We'll try to forget the fact that she shares her credit card with her husband, so therefore would not only be buying herself something but also paying for that gift herself. Or at least half of it.)

So, tell your friends who do the Valentine's Day Rant to not even bother wasting their breath. They'll need to save it for Mother's Day.

Celebuspawns

Toddlers of celebrities always look adorable and are well behaved in tabloid photos. You think these pint-size "sons and daughters of" are all on drugs. No toddler you know, including your own, is that adorable or well behaved all the time.

It was unfortunate, to say the least, that the one toddler I *just had* to bodycheck so my daughter could get a seat beside her best friend at a birthday party was Nevis.

Yes, Nevis. You know, *Nelly Furtado's daughter*.

It was unfortunate because I love Nelly Furtado. (I have all your songs on my iPod! I swear!)

Okay, so I'm slightly exaggerating. I didn't exactly bodycheck Nevis. It was more of a nudge. In my defense, I was just being proactive. I'm pretty sure Nelly Furtado would have bodychecked my daughter if she knew that her daughter just *had* to sit beside her best friend, or would end up having a complete meltdown at a very lovely birthday party. And I'd understand!

It was also unfortunate that it was Nelly Furtado's toddler because I'm a bit of a celebrity whore and I kind of wished my daughter could have become fast friends with Nevis, so I could become fast friends with Nelly Furtado and then meet Timbaland and go to the Grammy Awards.

If only I had offered Nevis a chair, instead of stealing one from her, Nelly would have thanked me and we'd be partying together right now.

I'm the kind of person who has a completely irrational belief that my daughter would get on really well with the toddlers of celebrities like, let's say, Courteney Cox Arquette (just like I have the completely irrational belief that *if I just got to meet* Jennifer Aniston in person, we'd become best friends and start tanning together at her beach house in Malibu).

Nelly Furtado, I am happy to say, seemed like a very normal mother. She was dressed in a sweatshirt and jeans (and trust me, some mothers show up to birthday parties dressed as if they were going to walk down a red carpet). She helped her toddler eat cake. She cheered when her daughter hit the piñata.

Nelly and Nevis seemed like most moms and 3-year-olds at a kid's birthday party.

Which was reassuring.

Thanks to tabloid magazines, I was starting to think that the toddlers of celebrities are all on some sort of drug (a drug, mind you, that I should definitely be on).

I'm not embarrassed to admit that I used to love *People* magazine and *US Weekly*. I'd read them religiously. If you're reading this (and good for you!), you're most likely the mother of a toddler and maybe a mother two or three times over and, well, kudos to you for finding the time to pick up a book with words that don't include, "Goodnight moon. Goodnight room. Goodnight cow jumping over the moon."

US Weekly, at the end of a long day, is the only thing my Mommy Brain can handle. Tabloid magazines are like picture books for adults. Most days, my brain can take in colors and photos and short captions like, "Kate Bosworth at an after-party!" or "Brad Pitt gets off his motorcycle" or "Gwyneth Paltrow buys toilet paper!" and that's about it.

And I love to read! Or at least I remember the days when I used to love to read. I used to stay up all night sometimes reading a good novel, but those days are long gone, even if I'm really into the novel. I know that in six short hours I'll have to get up, and sleep has become my number-one priority.

That's why *US Weekly*, *People* and *Hello!* are the perfect things to read before bed. They're short and you don't feel compelled to finish the story about Britney's new hair extensions before you nod off.

Needless to say, I've become somewhat of an expert on celebrities and their toddlers since I've become a mother.

I'm especially obsessed with the pages that scream, "Celebrities and Their Babies!" Or "Celebrity Moms' Day Out!" Or, "Daddy's Little Girls!" alongside photos featuring Ben Affleck and Brad Pitt with their daughters sitting on their shoulders, walking through a park.

I also really used to like the pages titled, "Stars!—They're Just Like US!" (There's Kate Moss with a flat tire! There's *Desperate Housewives*' Marcia Cross opening a bag of chips with her teeth! There's Hayden Panettiere getting a parking ticket! There's Lindsay Lohan buying groceries!)

But stars aren't just like us.

And not only because they have fame, money and wear sunglasses bigger than their faces.

Stars, from the look of it, are most definitely not "just like us" especially when it comes to being the mothers of toddlers.

Tabloid magazines *never* show photos of celebrity kids who don't look like the best-behaved, most adorable kids in the world.

You never see Suri Cruise, for example, looking anything but adorable and happy. You never see Gwen Stephani's son, Kingston, having a bad hair day. And he's only 2! And even though Angelina Jolie and Brad Pitt have friggin' *four* kids, they're always at a toy store, taking carriage rides in New York City or going to the circus. Not one of their four children is ever pictured grabbing on to either of their legs, with tears down their faces, while mom and dad look like they're going to cry, too.

I honestly believe tabloid magazines should have a two-page spread called, "Celebrity Parents: They're Just Like US!" and show

Maddox, Pax, Shiloh and Zahara having meltdowns, screaming on the floor, "I want more ice cream!" or, "No! I want another toy!" or, "I don't like you anymore!"

I *want* tabloids to feature Kingston yanking a fistful of his mother's hair while Gwen yelps out in pain, and says, "Do NOT pull my hair! I told you not to PULL MY HAIR!"

I want to see Ryan Phillippe and Reese Witherspoon's kids not smiling and being pushed on a swing in a playground, but grabbing a toy shovel from another kid's hand while Ryan and Reese scream out, "SHARE! SHARE!" as Ava throws sand in another kid's eyes.

That's reality! That would be "Just Like US!" And I'd way rather see that than read how Jennifer Garner "balances it so well, you never know how she does it." Why don't we ever see Suri Cruise, for god's sake, with food on her face? Why don't they show a photo of Angelina Jolie in a washroom changing Shiloh's diaper after a meal of peas? Why don't we see Heidi Klum and her brood looking anything less than perfect? Why can't we see Henry smacking his sister in a sibling-rivalry moment?

That, dear tabloid editors, would make me feel that "Stars Are Just Like US!" That would make me not want to stop buying your magazines because I think it's false advertising. Yes, it's false advertising.

When I see only happy, spotless, well-behaved celebrity kids walking around with their relaxed, well-dressed, smiling parents, I'm left thinking they're all on drugs. They must be. Because no toddlers are ever that well behaved. And no mother always looks that laid-back. So, celebrity mothers, can you let the rest of us know about these magic pills?

Too Much Information

These conversations make you realize having a second child is open for public debate, even if you barely know the debaters.

My brother and sister-in-law were visiting from their home in Israel this summer with their 2-year-old son. Their toddler is an adorable boy, with long, curly blond hair and big blue eyes. In fact, he's super adorable because he doesn't speak English. There's really nothing cuter than a 2-year-old speaking baby talk in Hebrew. (Except for those toddlers who have British accents. They're friggin' really adorable.)

My sister-in-law has many sisters and they all have many children.

When they were in town, we all headed up to my parents' cottage for a family weekend. My sister-in-law, who is very funny, kept walking around saying, "I have this big house and only one child. Poor me."

She wanted very badly to have another baby, but for some reason (okay, I completely get all the reasons) my brother has been holding off. He's not exactly into having a second child just yet.

"I have this big house and only one child. What's the point of having a house if you can't fill it with lots of children?" my sister-in-law would say every hour.

I found it quite interesting that she was so open about her desire to have a second child—even more so that she let it be known to all of us that my brother was the only thing (and kind of the most important thing—you know, his sperm and all) holding her back.

I felt kind of uncomfortable about the whole thing. I couldn't remember anyone else being so open about wanting a second child, to the point of telling everyone—over BBQ hamburgers and corn on the cob—that the reason she wasn't pregnant again was because of her husband/my brother. It was a unique experience, that weekend.

That was until a couple of weeks later when I was at a dinner party—a family dinner party, which means four couples with five kids—and the conversation came up again.

"We might be getting a dog," this woman Shelly announced to the table, as our kids were upstairs putting all the toys onto the couch.

"Oh, really? I love dogs. What kind are you getting?" I asked.

"Oh, I don't know," she sighed.

For someone getting a dog, she didn't seem very excited. She seemed disappointed.

"You don't seem very excited," I told her. "Are you not a dog person?"

"No, I like dogs. But I want another baby and my husband won't let me. His compromise is to get a dog." She sighed again.

And it wasn't as if her husband wasn't right there at the table. He was. He was right there listening to this conversation, saying, "I like small dogs."

When did it become okay for women to tell a table of people, or in-laws at cottage family weekends, that they want a second child, but their husbands are holding them back?

It happens a lot now. At a friend's house one night, another guest asked my friend if she was going to have another baby. (You learn that, even three weeks after having your first baby, people will start asking if you're going to have another.)

"We're in discussion about it right now," my friend answered.

"We're discussing it," her husband said. "Just in discussion."

This type of conversation puts people in a very awkward position, especially if you're already a parent.

When a woman gets something into her head, she gets it into her head. This I know. If I get it into my head that I want a pair of boots, the feeling will not go away.

I have often thought about having a second child. But then I remember how tired one of my friends was after having a second child when her first child was only 2. She was so tired one day at the post office that she left the post office and got into her car to drive to Starbucks for a triple shot of espresso.

But the craving for a triple shot of espresso didn't prove how tired she was. What proved how exhausting it was to have two kids was the fact that she got a call on her cellphone moments after she left the post office. It was a very nice woman who worked at the post office, where my friend had just filled out her change-of-address forms (and luckily had to include her cell number).

"Did you forget something?" the woman asked my friend.

"Did I?" she asked back.

"Yes, your baby," the woman at the post office said dryly.

Yes, my friend forgot her newborn at the post office. He was just sleeping in his car seat when she raced back in to get him.

(I'm not supposed to tell anyone this story because my friend worries her husband will get pissed. So please don't repeat it, especially after you read what follows.)

You'd think, considering my friend had just forgotten her baby at the post office, she would have learned her lesson. But she didn't. Ten minutes later, at Starbucks, she was paying for her triple shot and having the feeling that she'd left something behind. It hit her that she had left her baby in the car. Two times in twenty minutes. Not good.

The newborn sleep deprivation staged passed, and she now

remembers both her kids. Her son is adorable. So I can see why people want more than one child.

But it's never good to pick sides if you find yourself caught in one of these debates. It's like how you learn never to tell a friend that her guy sucks after they break up. There's always the chance they'll get back together and then you'll be the friend who complained about the boyfriend. Similarly, you don't want to list all the reasons it's good to "stick to one," for fear it will come back to bite you in the ass a few months later.

Besides, I think it's an argument best saved for behind closed doors. In your own home.

Not that it matters anymore—at least in my family's case. My sister-in-law is pregnant.

If I think about the timing, not that I really want to, she convinced my brother sometime between going fishing and eating watermelon.

The Other Parents

Like the bad joke, you will think, "How many parents does it take to change a light bulb?" Grandparents, after all, sometimes act as though they are your child's parents. They discipline them when they shouldn't, or don't when they really, really should.

The other night, I went out for probably the most unromantic dinner ever. This place made McDonald's look romantic. My dining companions were my toddler, my parents and my in-laws. There would be no sweet nothings whispered across candlelight, no hand holding under the table.

The restaurant—the Rainforest Cafe—is mammoth. It took about seven minutes, weaving around dozens upon dozens of tables, to be led to our table. Every fifteen minutes or so, the fake animals on the wall start howling and grunting. And, every half hour, a fake thunderstorm starts. There was a monkey on the wall over my chair, whose eyes I was convinced were looking into my heart. And the place was full of kids of all ages. (What's up, by the way, with the people who go to places like this but who don't have kids? Why would anyone do that to themselves?)

As I was eating my Buffalo chicken salad, I had this odd feeling that my toddler wasn't actually mine—that I wasn't her mother. I've had this feeling many times before. It always happens when my parents or the Fiancé's parents are around.

If you are someone's kid, you will *always* be their kid, which is why my mother still asks me, now that I've reached the age of 33, if I have to go to the bathroom before I leave her house. It's why my mother still reminds me that I should buy more toilet paper, even if I already have twenty-four rolls under the sink. It's why my mother still tells me, when I'm about to travel, not to forget my passport.

In my mother's eyes, I'm still 6.

But when you actually become a mother, you'd think that people—and by people I mean your own parents—would treat you as a mother, not a 6-year-old.

This doesn't happen. At the best of times, your parents will treat you like a 6-year-old mother.

I've gotten used to all the reminders from my parents and the In-laws, regarding my toddler like, "You'd better sign her up for dance classes!" "Did you sign her report card and bring it back?" and, "Do you think she needs a haircut?"

My toddler, still on her "I eat only food that is white" diet, ordered pasta with butter. There was a moment—sometime after the thunderstorm but right before the monkey above my head started to screech—when my daughter put both her hands in her bowl of pasta, like she was tossing a salad.

I didn't even bother to say, "Girl! Use a fork!"

I was with my in-laws and my parents and I knew, without a shadow of a doubt, they would take care of a situation. After all, they are the Other Parents.

I was right. All at once, all four of my daughter's grandparents started reprimanding her.

"Ah, Rowan! Don't do that!" "Use a fork!" "You're a big girl now! Don't use your hands!"

I sat there silently, trying to enjoy my salad. Of course, my daughter started to cry. It's one thing to be yelled at by one parent, but to be yelled at by four people at the same time—people who are usually, "I love you so much. Are you not just the prettiest girl in the whole world?"—put her over the edge.

I should also probably mention that it was my daughter's

birthday. Which is why we were at this Rainforest Cafe. We had already done the birthday party for her friends, the family birthday party at home and the party at her pre-school. But this was Monday night, her actual birthday.

Trust me. I don't like watching my daughter pretend her food was finger paint. But because I knew the Other Parents were around—other adults who by pure relations have a stake in her upbringing—I really did just sit there minding my own business.

She finally stopped crying and picked up a fork. I finished my salad. It was dessert time. We had asked our waiter to bring out a bowl of vanilla ice cream with a candle in it and asked for all the waiters to come sing "Happy Birthday" (it's that type of place).

Three waiters sang to her (loudly, if somewhat bored-ly) as the bowl of ice cream arrived.

She blew out the candle and then proceeded to stick her hands into the bowl, making "ice cream soup" with her fingers.

I kind of looked up at my in-laws and my parents, expecting them to yell at her. I realized, though, that after the last time they yelled at her all at once and she cried, they weren't going back there.

I would have to be the Parent. Ice cream is really sticky.

"Rowan! Use a spoon. You're a big girl now. Use a spoon!" I told her.

My parents and my in-laws all gasped at me in horror.

"Oh, leave her alone," they all cried at me. "It's her birthday!"

You've got to be kidding me, I thought. Why am I in trouble for telling *my own daughter* to use a spoon and not act like an animal? You guys just yelled at her for the same thing!

But there you have it. When you are a parent, and you are around your own parents, you are still a kid. You can't, god forbid, act like a parent.

One of my friends says her mother acts like her children's

mother, too. "She's always trying to get them to behave and tell them they shouldn't do this or shouldn't do that," my friend tells me.

My friend is brave. She actually says, "Mom, you don't have to discipline them. That's my job. You don't have to play that role."

Her mother, however, can't seem to stop. And her mother-in-law, my friend says, is worse. "She is convinced, even though she sees her grandchildren only a couple of times a month, that they're not getting enough vegetables. She'll literally follow them around the house trying to shove broccoli and cauliflower into their mouths," my friend says.

I shouldn't have been surprised when my parents demanded my toddler put on her coat and zip it up because it was chilly outside, before I even got the chance to open my mouth. Anyway, I'm pretty positive that if I had told her to do up her coat, the Other Parents would have yelled at me.

That's just the way it goes. When the Other Parents are around you are the Parent on paper only.

And you are still 6.

"Becky, do you have to go to the washroom before we leave?" my mother asked.

Shoot me. Shoot me now, I thought.

Straw Wars

These are the fights you find yourself getting into with toy packages and apple juice straws. You'll realize that toy manufacturers should put "adultproof" on boxes along with "childproof." It takes you forty-five minutes to open new toys and you have the five paper cuts to prove it. You need a manual to understand the manual.

My toddler drinks at least five apple juice boxes a day. Which means, at least five times a day, I feel like throwing the apple juice boxes against a wall—much like I feel about my alarm clock when it goes off after I've slept a total of three hours and have to go to the dentist for an 8 a.m. cavity filling.

I hate apple juice boxes. I can't open the damn plastic straw part. If there's one thing they shouldn't make childproof, it's the plastic straw covering of juice boxes. Parents have to open a hell of a lot of them.

My fingers are quite small and I still can't manage to open the damn things. I often end up trying to get the plastic wrapper off by banging the straw on the counter or using my teeth. Sometimes, later in the day, I find myself fishing out tiny pieces of plastic from between my molars.

The thing is, my toddler can open the straws! It doesn't seem to me to be so much a childproof device as an adultproof one. I actually feel like something is wrong with me when I can't open a damn apple juice straw. Especially when my daughter looks at me as if to say, "Just give me the damn thing already. I'll open it."

They're maddening, those apple juice boxes. But even more maddening are toddler toys that take two weeks to open.

"Can you open this, Mommy?" my toddler asked, about a birthday present she had received months ago. It was called a "Musical Carousel Coach."

I looked closely at the box and immediately hated the parent who bought this for my child. I hated that my toddler realized that the present hadn't been opened yet. The box read, "1,294 pieces included."

I looked at this Musical Carousel Coach with its princess pony and thought, "Okay, because I love you and you want to play with this, and because I wasn't smart enough to find a better hiding place, I'll open it."

I managed to rip open the box with a super sharp knife only to realize that all 1,294 pieces each had their very own ties at the back—ties that I would have to unwind, one by one.

I fucking hated this Musical Carousel Coach.

I began untying them all, with supplies. I had scissors handy. I had knives handy. I had screwdrivers handy. I was ready.

"This is taking a long time, Mommy," my daughter said after twenty minutes.

I was only halfway done. I was muttering under my breath, "What kind of super-kid could *ever* open this thing, *ever*? Not even Hulk Hogan could open this damn thing."

Toy companies do take children into consideration when packaging. They do not take impatient parents into consideration. Impatient parents like me, who after twenty minutes of unwinding wires that attach the toy parts to the box, then taking off individual plastic tabs, then taking off still more pieces of plastic, just want to toss the whole damn thing into the trash.

To make matters worse, every time I hit the box that this Musical Carousel Coach was in—out of sheer frustration—the toy would start making musical sounds. It was mocking me. I wanted to stab it with my scissors.

I hate packaging on behalf of all the trees that suffer. I hate it, too, because it is nothing short of maddening. Maddening is the only word that adequately describes opening children's toys these days.

And, then, sure enough, after you've spent close to an hour opening the toy packaging and you have five new paper cuts to prove it, your toddler, who all along was like, "This is taking a long time, Mommy," ends up playing with the thing for three minutes.

And then, of course, she'll ask for an apple juice box.

Instant Experts

This is the person you must become because your toddler's interests shift as quickly as the second hand on a clock. You must keep up with her newfound passions, even though you couldn't give a crap about the life cycle of a caterpillar or the different types of power tools.

I can remember a time, in the not so very distant past, when I had no idea who Dora the Explorer was. I remember it quite clearly. I was walking through Chinatown with a friend when she stopped and said, "I just want to run into this store. They have a Dora knapsack and I promised Solia that I'd buy her one."

I had a newborn, but I had no idea who Dora was.

"You don't know who Dora is? Oh, you will," this woman said to me. Little did I know.

These days, I have everything from Dora the Explorer toothbrushes to Dora bed sheets, to Dora dolls, Dora Band-Aids and Dora placemats. If *you* don't know who Dora is then you do not have a toddler. Or you live with your family under a rock.

Sometimes I'll be walking the street with a little ditty stuck in my head. And I'll be, like, "Where is that song from?" Then it will hit me. That little ditty going through my Mommy Brain is "D-D-D-Dora, D-D-D-Dora" from the theme song of *Dora the Explorer*, of which I own no fewer than 100 DVDs. And I'll want to bang my head on the concrete sidewalk.

When you have a child, you become an Instant Expert. Rather, you are forced to become an Instant Expert on whatever they are interested in. Now, I didn't mind the Dora the Explorer phase, because Dora would sometimes speak in Spanish. Thanks to this children's show. I now know how to count to ten in Spanish and can properly use words like "vamanos!" (It means, "Let's go!")

Thanks to Dora, I've also learned that toddlers really take in the things they see on television. When my daughter's flashlight broke, she said, "We'll have to put it through the super-fix-it machine."

And I'm, like, "What's a super-fix-it machine?"

"From Dora," she said. If she knew how to roll her eyes, she would have. "They put the boot with a hole in it through the super-fix-it machine and it was all fixed," she explained.

"Ri-ight. Of course," I said. "We'll have to put it through the super-fix-it machine." Obviously, I had to pay more attention.

But just when I literally became an expert in all things Dora— including the super-fix-it machine—my daughter decided she was done with Dora. Just like that. Poof. Interest gone. One day she loved Dora, the next she's all, "I don't like Dora anymore."

My daughter next became interested in Strawberry Shortcake. Which meant I had to become an Instant Expert in everything Strawberry Shortcake, including which one was Rainbow Sherbet, which one was Blueberry Muffin, everything there was to know about Strawberry Land, and that the cat was named Pupcake and the dog was named Custard. (Or is it the other way around? I can never remember.)

My toddler would get mad at me if I made a mistake. "That's not Orange Blossom! That's Rainbow Sherbet!" she'd say to me, to which the only reasonable response was, "Okay! Sorry! Excuse me for living!"

Then she was off Strawberry Shortcake and into Toopy and Binoo, who are two mice or rats, or some kind of rodents. For the longest time, even though there are only two characters, I couldn't get straight which was Toopy and which was Binoo. Frankly, I didn't give a crap.

But because my daughter was into Toopy and Binoo, I had to become an Instant Expert on all things Toopy and Binoo. I had to know which one was Toopy and which one was Binoo.

As bad as this is, it's worse for my friends with boys. They have to become Instant Experts on things like Bob the Builder, super-heroes, engines and sports.

Snooze. Yawn.

"When my son was 3 he was obsessed with superheroes and Power Rangers. I'd be playing with him saying, 'Okay, now this Power Ranger is about to rob a bank,' thinking, 'God, I just want to take a nap.' You are lucky you have a girl," my friend moaned to me.

It got even worse for my friend once her son became interested in construction. "I seriously had to learn what a Bobcat was and what a front-end loader was," my friend told me.

She even went out and bought three children's picture books on construction. Not for her kid. She bought them for herself—kind of like buying the Coles Notes version of *Sense and Sensibility* (or whatever book you didn't read in high school)—so she could cram and become the Instant Expert on construction.

You learn you have no choice. You must keep up. You must become an Instant Expert. Especially when your 2-year-old, who's into dinosaurs, suddenly says to you, "No, Mommy! *T. rex* was a carnivore. Triceratops is a herbivore." Suddenly you feel like a fucking idiot for not knowing all the names of each dinosaur and which were plant eaters and which were meat eaters. You spend an hour after putting your child to bed googling dinosaurs because your 2-year-old shouldn't know more than you.

Now my friend's son, who is 5, wants a potato gun. "Do you think there's some site on the Internet that will teach me how to make a potato gun?" she asked me recently. She wanted to look like a rock star to her child, even though she is anti-guns. She just wants her son to look at her and think, "My Mommy knows everything."

For a while there, I had to know the names of all the Wiggles. I bought the concert tickets, knowing full well that the day of the concert would be my worst nightmare come true.

The day before the concert, when I reminded my toddler with fake enthusiasm that, "We're going to the Wiggles tomorrow! Yay!" she decided she no longer liked the Wiggles, even though she did . . . yesterday.

I should have been grateful, but I was pissed off. We'd spent money on the Wiggles! I was so pissed off that I said, "We're going anyway. And we're going to enjoy every damn minute of it!" (Moral: be careful what concerts you buy tickets for, because by the time the concert comes around, your kid may no longer be interested.)

As an Instant Expert, you're left thinking to yourself, "What am I going to do with all this newfound knowledge on dinosaurs and chestnuts and turtles?"

The answer will come.

"I need to have another child!" you'll suddenly realize in a moment of insanity. Why should I let every song I've remembered, every rhyme I've learned, and this encyclopedic knowledge of turtles go to waste?

And maybe that's the true reason that people have second kids. They just don't want to waste all the hours spent learning about the life cycle of a caterpillar.

Plus One?

Are the kids invited to the party, or not? Their names aren't on the invitation. It must be a mistake. Or is it?

Sometimes even the most gracious, kind-hearted, kid-loving parents don't want your children around.

While you may be thinking, "Of course they *like* kids. They *have* four of them!" there will be certain instances when your children will not be welcome, even though the gracious, kind-hearted hosts, who have four kids of their own, will never come right out and say this to your face.

It's hard to tell when you get an invitation, sometimes, if it's appropriate to bring your children along. It's just like during those pre-kids years, when you got invitations stating dress codes like, "Runway Ready," or "Dress to Impress" and you were left wondering what the hell to wear and why invitations never just say, "Jeans and a cute tank top will be fine, don't worry about it." That's all you wanted to know anyway.

Invitations need to be more specific, especially for people who have children.

Honestly, parents really have to read between the lines. And all because your adult friends who invite you to anniversary parties, or 40th birthday bashes, or even lunches, won't ever put on the invitation, "I'll fucking kill you if you bring your kids."

People aren't even brave enough to write, "Kids not welcome."

I miss the days when an invite said, "BYOB" and you knew that it meant to bring your own booze. Later, BYOB turned into "Bring Your Own Baby," which, granted, was less fun than the old BYOB.

But at least you knew what you were supposed to bring: booze . . . or your baby.

So, the next time an invitation lands in your mailbox or inbox or wherever you normally receive invitations, take a hint:

1) If the invitation says, "Adults only," do not bring your kids.
2) If the invitation goes something like, "Come celebrate Brad's 40th birthday. Get a baby-sitter. There will be cocktails. Get a baby-sitter. And finger foods. Get a baby-sitter. Can't wait to see you all. Get a baby-sitter. Love ya!" do not bring your kids.
3) If you're talking to a friend a couple of days before a party and he says, repeatedly, that his own kids will be sleeping at their grandparents' place, do not bring your kids.
4) If you are trying to get your friend to tell you if toddlers are welcome and she says something like, "Well, *my* kids will be around because they *live here* and they have nowhere else to go," and they stress the "my" and "live here" parts, do not bring your kids.

Some parents don't understand all of this. "I almost killed my sister-in-law," one of my friends told me after her husband's birthday party. "I specifically told her there would be no kids there, and that she should get a baby-sitter, and she still showed up at my door with her three children. It changes the mood of the room," she continued. "You just want to get drunk and then you have to worry about making sure the kids are happy."

All parents, including me, get invites with just their names on the envelope and yet we still find ourselves asking, "I wonder if they just forgot to put our children on the envelope? Could this be a mistake?" Even though we know it would be more fun without our kids there, or if we were already planning on getting a sitter, we still get a little miffed that the kids' names weren't included.

Now, many families have gotten into decades-long fights because one family member didn't invite another family member to their bar mitzvah twenty-three years ago (seriously, what 4-year-old would really want to go to a bar mitzvah anyway?).

Not so long ago, I found myself somewhat miffed that my daughter wasn't invited to a Christmas brunch. The brunch was in someone's house—a relative!—on a Sunday at noon. Did I mention that it was for Christmas—the season of giving?

I didn't go. I told the Fiancé that I was offended beyond belief that my toddler wasn't invited, especially since the host's own grandkids were going to be there. And it was brunch, and it was on a Sunday and it was Christmas.

"Who are you kidding? You just don't want to go," he said.

Which was completely true. But I also thought it was rude. I mean, I have a toddler. We're a package deal.

There's another side to this story. As a parent, I'm super careful about inviting people over who don't have kids. I make sure they understand that there will be little people running around. "Remember, there will also be kids here," I'll say. "Are you sure you still want to join us for dinner?"

Even when they say, "Yes, I'll come. I understand there will be kids," I'll still say, "Are you sure you understand? There will be kids! Actual real-life kids! It will not be relaxing!"

The point? We all learn (hopefully) to spell. If we could just learn to spell things out, there would be a lot less confusion—about what to wear, and whether or not our toddlers are invited.

The Hostess with the Mostess

Thank god your child's birthday comes just once a year. The only thing worse than attending birthday parties, weekend after weekend, is actually hosting one. It's a competitive world out there.

Okay, all you future mothers out there—listen to me: Procreate in the month of December. Are you listening? Have a lot of sex in December! If you get it right, your baby will be born in September.

Sure, you say, that means I'll be at my most pregnant through the hot summer months. Why would I want to go through that?

Because, my friend, you're not looking into the future.

In the future lie birthday parties. And trust me, you want your child to be born at the start of the school year so you don't have to compete with the other birthday parties. You want to be first.

If you're not first, you are fucked when it comes to originality. You have to worry that your chosen venue is "been there done that." You have to worry that there has already been face painting, balloon clowns, the cooking birthday party, and the reptile birthday party. If your toddler's birthday is in April or May, you're doomed to be the parent who has to copy what's already been done.

Thankfully, my daughter's birthday falls early in the school year. I realized what a plus this was after I threw her what I thought was a very successful third birthday party at a dance school. All the kids had fun. They ate pizza. They got loot bags.

By the end of October, one month after school started, we had seen the clowns, the magician and the face painter. By November, all the invitations I received said, "Parents can stay for wine. Gifts can be donations to charity."

Birthday parties are competitive. You bring gingerbread cookies for all of your daughter's classmates, and another mother brings fifty helium balloons and gorgeous cupcakes. You thank god that you came first, because the next mom up will be forced to bring not only helium balloons and gorgeous cupcakes but something else. Maybe a striptease, so she can be the "memorable" parent (or the parent who "just doesn't care" as much).

The only thing worse than being invited to birthday parties—weekend after weekend, month after month—is the one day a year when you have to throw your toddler a birthday party and be the "hostess with the mostess."

When Rowan was 2, we went to a birthday party at an indoor gym. "This is a fun place," I told the mother of the birthday boy. "Maybe I'll book Rowan's birthday here in a couple of months."

"In a couple of months? You'll never get this place. It books up months and months in advance," she told me. "I've been planning his party for six months now."

Yes, the world of children's birthday parties has changed. No longer do you get handwritten cards telling you whose party it is, where to go, and when to go there. Instead, you get a stuffed animal with the invitation tied to a bow around its neck, or a china teacup in a box. You have to send out thank-you cards afterward. You have to plan "for months."

For the first two years of my daughter's life, I threw her birthday parties at home. This is a mistake. First, you have to worry not only about food for kids, but also food for adults. You have to plan entertainment and decorations. You have to clean up before the guests arrive and after they leave.

And, you have to worry about your kid, who is crying, while simultaneously worrying if all the other kids are having fun. (Did I mention that Rowan spent her first two birthday parties in tears, because at that age she was guaranteed only to be happy at

7:30 a.m., and you can't have a kids' birthday party at 7:30 a.m. Or can you?)

One year—after talking to a balloon maker who wanted to come over before the party for a "sit-down" discussion about how to decorate—I swore I'd never do it again. I blew off the balloon-maker, thinking, "Just put some helium balloons up and make balloon animals for the kids." Holy crap! It wasn't as if I were planning a wedding or anything!

But be careful. This is exactly what it might end up feeling like.

Recently I received a birthday invitation that I thought looked quite normal, until I read the line at the very bottom: "Valet parking."

Yes, this is what you'll be competing with.

But here's the thing about toddlers (and if you don't listen to anything else, please listen to this). A toddler has *no idea* if you've spent $3,000 on a birthday party with caterers, a balloon-animal maker, a face painter and a sketch artist (yes, that was us) or if you rent a dance school in a church basement, order pizza and have three teenagers teaching them dance moves (that was us after I learned the hard way). The cheaper and shittier the pizza, the better.

The toddler will still have a good time. This is because, when you're 2 or 3, you don't need much to make you happy. A $10 cake from the grocery store tastes as good as a $500, three-tiered cake.

And when it comes to the presents? Let's just say you realize how disgusting consumerism truly is when you get presents for your toddler's birthday. No kid needs twenty-one new toys in one day. And no one has room for twenty-one new toys. But if you invite twenty-one kids, that's what happens. You get twenty-one gifts. (I was once invited to a birthday party for a 4-year-old with sixty kids. You should have seen the gift table.) After Rowan's second birthday party, I didn't have to buy her a toy for a full year. I just put all of the presents away and every six weeks or so, I'd give her one.

One mother I know has a good rule. Her son can open all the presents he receives, but he can keep only three of them. The rest go to charity. This exercise not only teaches her toddler about giving back but also makes him think about what he really wants. (All of this is not to say that kids shouldn't get presents. They absolutely should! It's one of the joys of having a birthday. In fact, after thirty, it's the only joy.)

Some parents try to cope with consumer guilt in other ways. I once received an invitation that asked for us to bring a non-perishable food item to give to charity. That's not to say we weren't also supposed to bring a gift. But, for a brief moment, I thought, "Hey! This kid is getting a can of beans for her birthday! And, if she's lucky, a can of corn niblets as well."

Which, actually, wouldn't be the end of the world to a toddler.

I know I can't give a 3-year-old a can of pork beans. But, if most toddlers are like my daughter, they enjoy the act of ripping open presents more than they do the present themselves.

For my daughter's third birthday, she received great gifts. Amazing gifts. Except the one from a forty-year-old bachelor friend of ours. You know people like this, I'm sure. Child-free friends who have no concept of what an appropriate gift for a 3-year-old is. You know this because they show up with a gift that, right on the box (in big, bold letters), contains this warning: "Not appropriate for children under the age of 11."

I had to laugh. "It says right here, not for kids under age 11. She just turned 3!"

"I know," he said, grinning. "But it looks so cool, I just had to get it for her." (You may say, as I did, "Well, firecrackers are cool, too, but I'm not giving one to my toddler!")

Anyway, with mountains upon mountains of gifts, the thing

Rowan liked the most was . . . a birthday card, shaped like a castle, from my sister-in-law.

She played with that birthday card, opening it and closing it hundreds of times, for almost a week. (In Toddler Land, playing with the same thing for a week is like owning the same car for twelve years.)

So, maybe, just maybe, I could get away with giving a kid a can of pork beans or tuna. As long as I wrap it, that is. And get a good card.

Anti-Children Assholes

These non-parents act as though you've just walked into their store or restaurant holding hands with a cold sore, not a toddler. They don't even try to disguise their contempt. No shirts, no shoes, no toddlers.

I'm not saying my toddler is an angel 100 percent of the time.

I would *never* say that.

It's only 100 percent true that she is so *not* an angel 100 percent of the time.

Just last night, for example, my toddler emptied a twenty-five-pound bag of kibble onto the kitchen floor. Ruby, our eight-pound dog, was, apparently, "berry hungry."

Of course, my 2-year-old didn't dump the bag into a bowl. She didn't even attempt to pretend that she was attempting to dump the bag into a bowl.

I told her she had to clean it all up *immediately*.

After a few very long, very excruciating minutes—as I eyed the second hand of the clock while watching my toddler pick up the kibble, one piece at a time—I came to the unfortunate realization that we could be sitting on the kitchen floor for six or seven *weeks* before the mess was all picked up.

I put her to bed.

When the Fiancé came home from work and walked into the kitchen, making crunching sounds with every step he took, he asked the very logical question, "Why the fuck is there dog food everywhere?"

Like I said, I already know my daughter is not an angel.

But she's *my* not-angel.

So when people complain about her actions, or roll their eyes at her not-so-angelic behavior, I get annoyed. In fact, I get down-right pissed off.

My toddler is my not-angel and I love her more than anything, so don't be complaining about her. Don't be rolling your eyes at her, if you know what I mean.

Yes, fellow parents, it's true. Walking and breathing among us are Anti-children Assholes. And I don't mean people who have decided that kids just "aren't for them" or those who'd rather stick to being someone's aunt.

There are actual people out there who *hate* kids. And when these people realize they are breathing the same air as a toddler, in the same room, bizarre things can happen. For example, Anti-children Assholes generally look as pained as if they'd just been told that they have contracted genital herpes . . . after having sex . . . one time . . . with someone they didn't even like all that much.

Don't get me wrong. I *get* that if you are on an eight-hour, overnight plane ride, stuck in the seat next to a screaming baby who has an earache, you may not, for those eight hours, enjoy babies all that much.

I *understand* if you are a waiter who gets stuck serving a family with four kids under the age of 6, all of whom keep knocking over their drinks while the mother keeps demanding "More napkins! More napkins!" every time you pass by. I understand you may not actually be thrilled about having that family seated in your section.

I have a friend who owns a breakfast diner. We used to eat there every weekend with our toddler because they served pan-cakes, the most child-friendly food invention ever.

Then one day—poof—the pancakes were off the menu. And that was the end of weekend breakfasts at that diner.

My friend, the owner, said he made the decision to take the pancakes off the menu because there wasn't enough room on the grill. But I know the decision was more likely made because too many families were bringing in their toddlers for pancakes.

I know this *for a fact*. I know it because he actually said, "We took the pancakes off the menu and now I don't get as many parents with kids. Thank god. That was brutal." And he's a father of two toddlers!

I get it. Kids are awful customers (and awful dining companions). They spill, throw food on the floor, pour salt all over the place and run around banging into things and people.

But *I'm* not an awful customer. Not when it comes to diners, and especially not when it comes to shopping. I'm a fucking fantastic customer when it comes to shopping. Just look at my Visa bill.

There was this one clothing store I used to (and you'll see in a minute why I use the words "used to") frequent all the time. They sell amazing, funky clothes and I always *used to* walk out with a heavy bag, grateful my credit card hadn't been declined. Then I had to sneak the bags into the house, for fear the Fiancé would see all that I had bought. Then I'd have to listen to him say something like, "Another pair of jeans? How many pairs do you need?"

That's what a great customer I was. *I had to sneak through the back door of my house after shopping at this store*. And I did. Happily.

Apparently, however, I made a grave mistake by taking my 2-year-old into this store with me one afternoon for a planned shopping spree.

Bringing your toddler along with you while you shop for clothes makes about as much sense as a Gamblers Anonymous group holding a meeting in a Las Vegas casino. It just can't end well.

As a mom, you already know this. But you can't stop yourself. Just because you have a child doesn't mean your shopping addiction goes away. You always convince yourself that *this time* it will be different, this time your child will behave. You convince yourself of this even though you know that you'd have a better shot at putting $1,000 on red and winning than your child actually behaving.

But some days you just desperately *need* retail therapy. You *need* to bring your toddler along with you. Sure, most likely, your child will end up running in and out of the change room at the exact moment your pants are off and your shirt is stuck around your head—but that's just part and parcel of bringing a toddler shopping with you.

Toddlers don't sit nicely on the bench in the change room and say, "Yes, that looks really great on you, Mom. You should definitely get that." Or, "No, Mommy, I think that makes your ass look fat."

So, on this one day at my ex-favorite clothing store, I had just finished trying on a bunch of clothes while my toddler was entertaining herself by running around, hiding in the racks of clothing, and yelling out, "Find me! You can't find me!"

She was being a not-angel. Yet, at the same time, she really was just being her 2-year-old self. I actually thought she was being pretty good. (This was not some fancy, high-end boutique, I should add. There was rock music blasting and the sales people all looked hungover.)

I had hundreds of dollars worth of clothing I planned to purchase. All I needed to do was walk up to the counter and pay for them.

I plopped the clothes on the counter, while fishing out my wallet, while praying my credit card wouldn't be declined, while thinking of ways to sneak the clothes into the house unnoticed.

My so-not-an-angel daughter, meanwhile, had found the sunglasses display and was spinning it around like it was a spinning top. And hey, why not? That's what adults do when we're looking at the sunglasses display. (Of course, we actually look at the sunglasses, instead of spinning the display around just to see how fast it can go.) The sales clerk looked at my daughter, who was crying out, "WHEEE!" and said huffily, "Can you get her to stop touch-ing the sunglasses display? She's getting fingerprints all over it."

This sales clerk didn't even use the *magic word*. Bitch.

I so did not like this woman. I especially didn't like the way she was looking at my daughter—as if she were a pus-filled white-head she woke up to see on the middle of her nose. Yes, that's how much disgust she had in her voice and eyes.

I looked at this sales clerk, biting my tongue, and thought, "Well *someone* certainly doesn't work on commission."

Then I thought, "And someone *certainly* doesn't have kids."

If she had had kids she would know that kids leave finger-prints. Everywhere. All the time. Wherever they go. Always. No matter what. Even when their hands are perfectly clean, toddlers somehow manage to leave fingerprints.

Are *fingerprints* really such a big deal—especially when I had a few hundred dollars worth of clothes I was about to purchase?

I felt a rush of anger race through me. "Get a fucking bottle of Windex out," I thought, "and a sheet of paper towel and wipe the fingerprints off." It would take, oh, I don't know, about thirty sec-onds. Just thirty lousy seconds of her life!

I had a choice to make. Did I stop my daughter from being a 2-year-old? Did I just buy the clothes and get the hell out of there without saying anything?

I was so torn. I absolutely adored the jeans I was about to buy (and so didn't need). I wanted those jeans I so didn't need. Badly.

But when it comes to being a parent, I realized at that moment, you always side with your child when strangers are rude about them—and especially when they don't use the *magic word* while being rude about them. And especially, when your toddler really wasn't being that bad. She was just being 2.

With a heavy heart, I said, "You know what? I don't need these," and walked out of the store, holding my not-so-angelic daughter's clean hand, with my head held high, leaving the perfect pair of jeans and the cutest tank tops behind. At least I still had my pride. Sort of.

"Anti-children Asshole," I thought to myself. "She just gave up a few hundred dollars in sales all because of some fingerprints on a sunglasses display."

I'm not the only mother who has dealt with this breed of anti-children people. One of my mother friends decided to take her three young children to a home furnishing store on a Saturday afternoon. Her three kids were running around and two-thirds of her offspring were having temper tantrums at the same time. "The salesperson followed us around the entire time sighing, 'Oh my god! Oh my god! Oh my god!' as if we were the worst parents in the world and as if my children were the most out-of-control kids they have ever seen and who were about to set fire to their store. They were just so unsympathetic," my friend told me. "It was the weekend. What did they expect us to do? I will never go back there."

I often wonder if that sales clerk at the clothing store regretted complaining about my toddler (just as often as, I'll admit, I fantasize about that perfect pair of jeans I left behind).

Unfortunately, having a run-in with Anti-children Assholes is a lose-lose situation. The store lost me as a customer (along with thousands of dollars in future sales), but I can no longer frequent my all-time ex-favorite clothing store. No one really wins.

And it just goes on and on. Remember when you were single, and you noticed how many people were in couples, or when you started to yearn for a baby and saw pregnant ladies everywhere you looked? Now that you're the parent of a toddler, you start to notice just how many Anti-children Assholes there are.

As of two weeks ago, I can also no longer frequent my favorite sushi restaurant with my toddler. I'm happy to say, though, that my toddler is not to blame. My friend Kama's toddler is to blame.

Her 2-year-old was a complete "devil child"—her term, not mine—one evening recently at this restaurant. We're talking three broken bowls, chopsticks flying across the room, waiters hiding for cover and pounds of rice on the floor.

The following night, a handwritten sign was posted on the front door announcing that no minors (anyone under the age of 18) were allowed in the restaurant. The owners even added, "Bylaw number 1835," which I have a feeling is a completely bull-shit bylaw. The owners just didn't want to have any more toddlers in their restaurant. (Again, I'd like to mention, this wasn't a five-star, white-glove, top-of-the-line-service restaurant. It was a dive of a sushi place.)

Another one of my friends was taking her toddler to another dive-like restaurant where they were meeting her parents and sisters for lunch. She, too, ran into Anti-children Assholes.

"We had our stroller with us," my friend told me. "When we walked in, the first thing the server said to us was, 'Sorry. We don't allow strollers in here.' The place was empty. I might understand if it was busy, but it was completely empty. Then I asked for a high-chair and the server said, 'We don't have highchairs,' and added, 'and we don't have a kids' menu either,' before he stormed off. They were literally doing everything in their power to not have us there. You know when the waitress is pouring from the coffee pot right over your kid's head that it isn't a child-friendly place," my friend said.

She, too, will never go back to this restaurant. Not that they want her there. At least not with her toddler.

When you have a child, you give up a lot. You give up your life! And when there are Anti-children Assholes out there, you give up a whole lot more you never would have expected to give up—like the perfect pair of jeans, or your favorite sushi restaurant.

The worst of it, though, is that anti-children-store or anti-children-restaurant owners don't seem to care about losing us parents as customers. Walking out of one of these places is like yelling at your boyfriend, "Get out of here," after he's already stormed out of your place, or saying, "I'm not talking to you," when your partner doesn't seem to notice that you're not talking to them.

Anti-children Assholes are only too happy to not ever see our toddlers again. So I take back what I said before. It's not really a lose-lose situation at all. The only ones who lose are parents. (Plus, I'm now too embarrassed to go back. My stance and all.)

If any of you Anti-children Assholes out there happen to be reading this (yeah, right), listen up. I'm not saying you have to like kids. I'm just asking that, even if you hate them, please just respect that we have them. And that just because we're mothers doesn't mean we don't like clothes and sushi. So, bite your tongues and take our money. Turn a blind eye to fingerprints. Just please let us shop and eat!

In the meantime, there's nothing we parents can do for revenge except to hope that one day, these Anti-children Assholes will have eight kids of their own and someone will say to them, "Can you get your brats out of here?"

Part VIII
Oh, No You Didn't!

Anna: I yike your earwings, Mommy.
Mommy: Thank you, Anna.
Anna: I yike your pretty neckyace.
Mommy: Thank you.
Anna: I yike your boobies.
Mommy: Thank you, Anna.

Anna, 3, daughter of Peggy Rust

"You're Not My Friend!"

The shocking sentence your toddler will inevitably yell at you. Your feelings are hurt. You so didn't deserve that!

I was once dumped, sort of, on my birthday.

At the time, I thought it was probably the most painful emotional experience of my life.

Dumping someone on her birthday is just plain mean, especially if you don't give her at least a pity present or consolation prize first.

I did get a present/consolation prize. It was a CD, possibly the most unromantic gift a gal can get after being in a relationship with someone for two years. Looking back, it was the kind of gift that screams, "I'm going to ditch you and if it wasn't your birthday today I'd do it right now, but because it is your birthday I'll wait until 12:01 a.m."

Which is kind of what happened.

But two weeks ago, that painful experience was trumped. Because the nastiest, most emotionally hurtful words ever were said to me—by my 2-year-old.

After that, being dumped on my birthday seemed like winning the lottery.

My toddler's exact words? "I'm not going to be your friend anymore!"

"I'm not going to be your friend anymore!" my daughter had huffed.

Hello, I thought. She did not just say that to me, did she?

My immediate reaction was to say, "First of all, I'm not your friend. I'm your *mother*."

My second thought was, "What did I do to deserve *that?*"

All I had said to her was, "Stop spilling your drink on the couch. Put your sippy cup on the coffee table."

I wanted her to stop spilling her drink on the couch. I wanted her to put her sippy cup on the coffee table.

It was a perfectly reasonable request, in my mind, and so not deserving of the response, "I'm not going to be your friend anymore!"

To add icing on the cake, my daughter even crossed her arms while telling me she wasn't going to be my friend anymore. She was all business.

She was not going to be my friend anymore. Huff.

I know. Ouch.

I was in too much shock from those hurtful words to say anything. Except, "I'm not going to be your friend either," while crossing my arms and asking myself, "Jesus. How old are you Rebecca?"

There's nothing like a 2-year-old to make you act like a 2-year-old.

So there was my toddler, with her arms crossed, scowling at me, and there I was, with my arms crossed, scowling at her. The sentence, "I'm not going to be your friend anymore" was ringing loudly in my ears. And through that sound, I think I could actually hear my heart crack a little.

My friend says she was "crushed" the first time her toddler said, "I don't like you."

"It really crushed me. But then she started saying it all the time, so now I just say, 'I don't like you either.'"

Sure, we all can't wait for our babies to speak. And, yes, it's super cute when they say, "mommy" or "milk" or even "penis" (especially when they say "pee-nuth"). But when they actually learn to speak in sentences and somehow know the exact words that will hurt you, well, it hurts. It hurts a lot. It really, really hurts. A lot.

Females know how much friendships mean. Friendships are everything to girls, to teenagers, to young women, to middle-age women, to women of all ages. Which is why it's so hurtful to hear your own daughter say, "I'm not going to be your friend anymore."

If you're a girl, that's one of the nastiest things you can possibly say to another girl, next to, "Okay, I did sleep with your boyfriend."

My daughter and I made up. I mean, as much as you can make up with a toddler. She stopped pouring her drink on the couch and put her sippy cup on the table, and I asked (kind of desperately, I'll admit), "Are we friends again?" and she said, "Yes." And then I said, "Okay, I'm your friend again, too."

And then we went back to watching *Dora the Explorer*. At least toddlers don't remain mad for long. In fact, I'm not sure which lasted longer: her not being my friend, or the sippy cup remaining on the coffee table.

I told the Fiancé, when he came home from work, what our daughter had said to me, and how badly it hurt my feelings.

"Do you remember what she said to me last night?" he asked, not as sympathetically as I expected or wanted him to be.

"Yes," I sighed. "I remember."

The Fiancé went up to our daughter's room to check in on her. She had been calling out for me, but I sent him up instead. (I was in the middle of watching *Grey's Anatomy*.)

When he walked into her room, she told him to "Go away."

Yes, our daughter actually told her own father to "Go away."

The Fiancé did. Happily. And then he went back to watching golf.

The Fiancé is not a woman, though. He didn't take it personally. He just took it literally and went away.

But I'm a girl and I take things personally—very personally. So when my daughter said to me, "I'm not going to be your friend anymore," I took it quite literally to mean that she didn't want to be my friend anymore.

I moped around the house for hours saying, "I can't believe she said she didn't want to be my friend!" while the Fiancé kept telling me "not to take it personally" and updating me on golf scores.

I soon realized he was right.

My toddler has said the dreaded words a number of times now.

I'll say, "Get into your pajamas," and she'll say, "I'm not going to be your friend anymore." Or I'll say, "Stop throwing your broccoli onto the floor," and she'll say, "I'm not going to be your friend anymore." Or I'll say, "Carrots are not for rolling under the stove," and she'll say, "I'm not going to be your friend anymore."

The phrase kind of loses its meaning once you hear it every day, twelve times a day, for a week. It's like the little girl who cries wolf. My daughter is the little girl and "I'm not going to be your friend anymore" is the crying-wolf part.

One of my friends tells me that I'm lucky. Her toddler says, "I hate you," which, I agree, is worse than, "I'm not going to be your friend anymore."

"I just want to kill her when she says that," my friend says. "After all I do for her! She hates me?"

I haven't yet heard, "I hate you." Yet. When I do, I know it will kill me. Just kill me.

At least I now have a new emotionally painful experience to wash away being dumped on my birthday.

I'm over that now. I am. I swear. Mostly anyway.

The Please Shut Up Moment

Your toddler does not have a verbal editing machine and sees no problem yelling out inappropriate statements in public. You wish the ground would swallow you up, or (at the very least) that you could muzzle your child without social services being called. You just want to yell, "Zip the lip!"

"Why is her hair like that?" my darling daughter says loudly.

We're getting manicures (they do toddlers at this walk-in place for $5) and sitting next to us—let me repeat, *next to us*—is a woman getting a pedicure. My daughter is pointing at her.

I ignore my toddler, pretending to be fascinated by my freshly painted nails. "Mommy! I said, 'Why is her hair like that?'" my daughter says again, this time louder and more huffily.

I don't understand why toddlers don't understand the concept of whispering. Even when they use their "indoor voices" or attempt to whisper, they still talk as loud as I used to talk to my grandfather before I realized he had put in his hearing aid.

I look up at the woman *next to us* and glance at her hair. Now, if my daughter was all, like, "Why is her hair like that?" and was pointing at a punk rocker with a rainbow-colored mohawk, I'd be less mortified than I am at this moment.

I would just tell her, "That's called a mohawk."

We've passed punks with mohawks on the street before and my toddler never seems interested. It's always me saying, "Look at that guy's purple spikes!"

Because, in my opinion, if you're going to dye your hair purple, you want people to notice you and point at you.

But this woman was not sporting a purple mohawk. This

woman—sitting as close to us as if we were on the same love seat—simply had her black hair died with a chunk of blonde at the front.

Yes, I'll admit, she kind of resembled a skunk. Personally, I didn't like her hair all that much either. But I knew this woman thought she would look really good with this type of highlight. She had probably gone to her hairstylist and discussed it. And really, she looked fine.

"I don't know," I told my daughter sternly, hoping she would get my tone, which said, "Shut up about this."

My daughter moved on. Yes, she did. She moved on from saying, "Why is her hair like that?" to saying, "I don't like her hair. I don't like her hair. Mommy? I don't like her hair."

Because I had no idea what to do, aside from silently asking god to please make my daughter shut up. I did say, "No, her hair is nice," I said this while looking at the woman, adding a shoulder shrug that said, "Kids! They're so dumb. They wouldn't know a good haircut if it bit them in the ass."

The woman smiled nicely, but I could tell she was slightly hurt.

Especially after my stubborn toddler, as I knew she would, responded, "No! It's not nice! Her hair is not nice!"

I wasn't going to get into it with my daughter while getting manicures. I didn't want to hurt this woman's feelings any more. Saying, "That's not a nice thing to say," would just bring more attention to the fact my daughter hated this woman's hair.

I just had to get out of the place ASAP, and then yell at my toddler when we were outside.

But my nails were still drying. If we left that instant, $25 would go straight down the drain. I started blowing on my nails furiously.

"I don't like her hair. Why is her hair like that?" my daughter said again.

Why couldn't she just let it go?

"Some adults like their hair like that. Maybe when you're a big girl you'll get your hair done like that," I suggested.

Sometimes pulling out the whole, "You're a kid and big people do different things," works.

Not this time. My daughter stomped her foot and said, "I'm NOT going to get my hair like that when I'm a big girl."

Again, I looked at this woman with a smile I hope said, "I'm just the baby-sitter. She's not mine!"

When you are living a Please Shut Up Moment, you get torn. I suppose I could have gotten into it with her and told her, "If you don't have something nice to say, don't say anything at all," but I'm not sure my toddler would get that. And plus, I *could* understand why she didn't like this woman's hair.

There have been other Please Shut Up Moments. Some were just as bad, some not so bad. I've handled situations better. Or maybe not. But at least I tried.

For example, when we passed a person in a wheelchair, my toddler used to ask, "Why is that person in a wheelchair?" The people we passed in wheelchairs were usually elderly people.

"Sometimes when you get older, you get tired. A wheelchair is like a stroller for old people," I explained.

Which was fine, until we passed someone in a wheelchair who was much younger.

"Why is that man in a wheelchair? He's not old," my daughter asked.

"Because sometimes people need help getting around. You know how I push you in your stroller? It's kind of the same thing." Luckily, this seemed to satisfy her, but it was also unfortunate for me. I was actually in the process of training my toddler to not use the stroller anywhere anymore and I didn't want her thinking that I would still be pushing her in her stroller when she was 10 and her feet were tired.

One of my friend's toddlers learned the word "fat," all because his grandmother was trying to get around a chair at a table and said, "I'm too fat."

My friend had to explain what fat meant, which was a mistake, because every time her toddler saw someone big he would scream, "That person is fat!"

Once, at a beach, a really obese man was walking by and her son said, "Mom, that man is really fat."

Which led my friend into a whole discussion about, "That hurts people's feelings and how would you feel if someone said that about you?"

At the same time, my friend said, "It was hard because the man really was fat. It was the truth."

Swear words come up a lot when I ask my mother friends about Please Shut Up Moments with their toddlers.

Nothing is funnier than my friend's toddler, who had a black eye after falling off his bed. For days after people would say to him, "Wow, that looks like it hurts. Does it hurt?"

My friend's toddler would always respond, "It hurts like a bitch."

It's worse when you have a Please Shut Up Moment around someone you know and like.

One of my best friends kindly invited me and my toddler over for a play date. I love going to my friend's house for a play date. She lives in a nice place, is friendly and usually feeds my daughter dinner.

My daughter was playing with one of my friend's kids when suddenly she announced, "I don't like Vita anymore! I don't want to play with her! I don't like her." Now, let me explain that my primary concern was not Vita's feelings. (Vita didn't seem to care at all that my daughter didn't like her at that moment) but the feelings of Vita's mother, who is one of my closest friends and also one of the nicest people I have ever met.

"Why doesn't she like Vita anymore?" my friend asked, while I was silently praying to god, "Please get my daughter to shut up."

In that instance, I certainly couldn't pretend that I was the baby-sitter, though I wanted to. I felt awful, much like I did when my daughter was saying, "I don't like her hair!" to the poor woman sitting next to us at the walk-in nail place.

But actually, this was worse. Vita's mom was a friend and not just some random woman getting her nails done whom I'd probably never see again.

I kept saying to my toddler, "Yes, you do! You like Vita! She's your friend!" to which my daughter kept saying, "I don't like Vita anymore!"

I would have yelled at my daughter and said, "That is rude. You do not say rude things, especially since Vita's mother was so nice to invite you over." But I knew that would just make her cry and I didn't really want to yell at my kid—who was in a totally non-understanding mood—in front of my friend.

It got to the point where I just had to take her home. As we backed out the front door, I stammered, "No seriously. She says she doesn't like people all the time now. It must be a phase! She even says she doesn't like me!"

On the way home, I asked my daughter, "Why don't you like Vita anymore?"

"Because I saw her underpants," my daughter answered.

What do you say to that? How do you reason with that?

There are too many Please Shut Up Moments to count.

At a pharmacy checkout, my daughter recently said about the East Indian cashier, "Mommy, why is she brown?"

Which forced me into explaining that people are born all different colors.

We had another "Please Shut Up Moment" recently. We were

walking on the street, and came to a stoplight. There was a gang of tough and rough-looking men standing at the corner.

It was the kind of group that, if it were dark, you'd cross to the other side of the street to avoid. One of the men threw an empty pop can onto the street.

"Mommy! Why is he leaving garbage on the street?" my daughter asked loudly.

"I don't know," I said, pressing the button furiously.

"Mommy! WHY IS HE LEAVING GARBAGE ON THE STREET?" she yelled.

Gang members do not see the humor in toddlers. This man, who definitely heard my toddler, did not even crack a smile.

We teach our toddlers that littering is a very bad thing and that they should never do it. We forget to tell them that littering is okay if it's a gang member who is leaving the garbage on the street—especially if Mommy is scared of the gang member, who looks as though he will kill you if you even look in his direction.

Eventually, you will have to explain to your toddler that they just can't go around yelling out their *opinions and feelings* on everything and anyone. They can't just *ask* certain questions in public. They have to keep their true feelings inside, like the rest of us.

The Look

This is the stare of utter disdain your toddler gives you for no apparent reason. You can't read it, but you know it says something like, "You're a moron, Mommy."

I know when my Fiancé is pissed at me when we're out in public because he'll give me the Look. It's a look that says, "We'll talk about this later." I know that look well. I understand that look.

We all look for looks to help us understand what someone is really thinking.

For example, if we are invited to a surprise party, we look at the guest of honor's face to see if they really are surprised or if their best friend already told them about the party and they're just pretending.

If we walk into someone by accident on the street before 9 a.m., they'll give us a look that says, "Screw you." We know what they're thinking without them having to utter the words.

The Fiancé can also tell if I'm mad at him by the Look on my face. "What did I do now? I can tell I did something wrong by the look on your face," he'll say.

To which I'll say, "What look? I'm not mad," to which he'll say, "I can tell you're mad." To which I'll then agree that I am mad and launch into whatever he did to make me have the Look on my face. It's good when you're an adult to have the Look, so your partner can know when he's done something wrong.

But my daughter sometimes has the Look. And I can't, if my life depended on it, figure out what it means. I have no idea what she's thinking when she gives me the Toddler Look.

I'll never figure it out, because she can't verbalize feelings just yet (as evidence I'll give you the fact that she says, "I'm mad" while laughing hysterically).

The Look that my toddler gives me actually sends shivers up my spine. It not only scares the life out of me but also makes me wonder, "What the hell is she thinking right now?"

Of course, unlike the men with whom we might have relationships, toddlers do not understand, "What are you thinking about right now?"

Which is good, in a way, because no man I've ever been with, or slept with, has ever seemed to like to answer that question. This is especially true after you've just had wild sex, and you're expecting him to say something along the lines of, "You have no idea how much I love you," when really he's probably not thinking anything at all or maybe just that he's kind of hungry. (Really. I do think that most men don't think anything at all after sex, unless they're thinking, "I wonder how far away the nearest Mr. Sub is?")

But, oh, the look my toddler gives me sometimes. It's a look, I swear, only a toddler can give. I have yet to see this kind of look on an adult's face. Ever.

It's a facial expression that is hard to explain. It's not like when I tell her, "No more marshmallows," and she pouts or her mouth turns upside down. I know she's about to cry. I know that look.

I know the look when she's sad that I'm going off to work. I know the look of her eyes lighting up when I tell her we're going to a party.

But the Look that comes out of nowhere, at no particular time of day, and appears for no rhyme or reason? That Look is evil. There's no other way of saying it. It would be the kind of look I would get, I suppose, if I told an adult that Hitler was a good guy. Of course, I would never say or think that, certainly not to a 3-year-old. And, yet, that is the Look my 3-year-old sometimes gives me, as if she is an adult and that is what I had just told her.

The only other explanation for this look is that she's thinking I just said the dumbest thing in the world. It's as if she's thinking, "Mommy, you're such a moron." But how could she be thinking that? She's only 3!

One of my mother friends who has both a son and a daughter thinks the Toddler Look is a girl thing. "When she was 2, my daughter would give me the look of death," my friend told me. "I would say something like, 'It's nice outside today,' and she'd just give me this look like I told her Barney hated her."

It's strange when a toddler can make you feel uncomfortable just by giving you the Look.

But I'm not going to ask, "What are you thinking about right now?"

I've asked that question too many times in my past. And I've never really been satisfied with the answer. Has any woman?

Toddler Rats

Your toddler can talk now, which means you have to start watching what you say. Your toddler will tattle. The Toddler Rat will repeat something you shouldn't have said about someone, to that very person. She won't even hesitate.

I don't like rats. (Or mice. Or spiders.)

But I really don't like rats, as in those who rat out others. In other words, I don't like tattletales. I especially didn't like it early one morning when my daughter ratted me out.

I couldn't believe she ratted out her own mother—the woman who carried her in her womb for nine long months, the person who loves her more than anyone else, the person who wipes her ass!

But this is what happens when your toddler can speak. They don't know what is appropriate to say and what's not appropriate to say. And I'm not talking about saying, "My vagina is itchy," in the middle of a grocery store.

And yes, the whole situation was my fault because I was the one who had opened my big mouth. But my daughter usually barely looks up at me—even if I'm tap dancing in front of her with a clown's nose on—when she's watching *Dora the Explorer*, which she was that morning.

How was I supposed to know that she was paying attention to what I was muttering under my breath? How was I to know she would use it against me?

Also, my daughter has the attention span of a flea. She can't remember what she ate three minutes ago, so how was I to know she'd remember, twenty minutes later, something I had said in passing?

This is what happened. We were going on a family vacation to Maui. Nanny Mimi had offered to pack our daughter's suitcase, which I happily agreed to, because I hate packing as much as I hate math. I can't do either very well.

But I do know one thing about Maui. It's hot there.

So, the morning our plane was leaving, Nanny Mimi was coming over to get our daughter ready so the Fiancé and I could pack our own luggage. As any parent knows, traveling with children takes a lot of thought and packing. Traveling with children on an airplane takes as much thought and packing as if you were moving for a year-long sabbatical.

Before Nanny Mimi arrived, I happened to peek into my daughter's suitcase, which was packed and in the kitchen. Nanny Mimi had packed about twelve sweat suits, five pairs of jeans and a bunch of other clothes I knew my daughter would never ever need in Maui. In Maui you need a couple of tank tops and a couple of bathing suits and you're good to go. You don't need mittens.

Because we'd had to get up at 5 a.m. to catch the flight, I was so not in a chipper mood.

I started unpacking the sweat suits from our daughter's suitcase—no, seriously, I thought to myself, why did Mimi pack winter boots?—and muttered, "Mimi is the worst packer ever!"

My daughter was watching television when I said this. Now, to be fair, Nanny Mimi isn't exactly the worst packer ever. She's an amazing packer, in the sense that she could fit a month's worth of clothing into one mini suitcase. I wish I had that skill. She just wasn't particularly skilled at picking the kinds of clothes needed to go into the suitcase for this particular tropical vacation.

Nanny Mimi arrived and that's when my darling daughter ratted me out.

She said to Nanny Mimi, "Mommy said you were the worst packer."

I felt my face go red and my heart stop.

"I did not say that," I protested.

"Yes you did! You said Mimi was the worst packer," my daughter said again.

What I wanted to say was, "When did you start paying attention to what I say, you little brat?"

But I felt a disaster on hand. I felt awful. Yes, I did say that Mimi was the worst packer, but it wasn't supposed to be heard by anyone—especially Nanny Mimi, whom I adore.

"No, I did not say she was the worst packer," I protested again. "You're being silly!"

"Yes you did!" my daughter screamed. "You said that Mimi was the worst packer."

And, then, of course, because I wasn't agreeing with her and it was early, she started to cry.

"You said Mimi was the worst packer ever! You said that Mimi was the worst packer ever!" she cried.

God, the Toddler Tattletale is the *worst*. Wasn't she supposed to be on my side?

I tried to get out of it. "No! I said she was a 'backpacker.' I said she was a 'backpacker!'"

Which was ridiculous.

Why would I ever say that my nanny was a backpacker?

Nanny Mimi is not an idiot. She's very smart (aside from packing snowsuits to go to Maui). Of course she knew that I had said she was the worst packer, thanks to my rat of a toddler. She knew I was just trying to get out of it and save face.

Needless to say, I felt awful. And I think Mimi felt awful, which made me feel even more awful. Nanny Mimi was good about it. She said to my daughter, "That's okay. Maybe I'm not a good packer."

To which my daughter said, "Mommy said you were the worst packer."

"Okay, enough. We get it!" I finally said. "We all heard you the first ten times."

I learned my lesson. Namely, that from then on, I couldn't complain about other people to her, or even while in the same room as her—and that I would have to buy Nanny Mimi an especially special gift from Maui.

There would be no more, "I can't believe Daddy is not home yet. Where the heck is he?" Or, "That kid in your class is ugly."

Because until my daughter can understand the concept of "Don't tell on your mother," I'll have to keep my trap shut.

Who knows when else she would rat me out?

And I am not alone. One of my best friends was in a fight with her husband. They were fighting in the car, with their toddler in the back seat. Her husband got out of the car to run to the bank machine. As soon as he'd slammed the car door, my girlfriend huffed aloud, "He's such an idiot!"

When her husband got back into the car thirty seconds later the Toddler Rat was all, "You're an idiot, Daddy. You're an idiot. Daddy's an idiot. Daddy's an idiot. You're an idiot, Daddy."

Luckily, her husband found this quite funny. Because her toddler ratted her out, they had a good laugh and made up. That's a happy Toddler Rat story.

Others are not so lucky. Another friend got into a fight with her mother-in-law after her daughter ratted her out.

"What's ammoying mean?" her daughter asked the grandmother. "Mommy says you're ammoying."

"Our relationship was strained, to say the least, for a few months after that. I definitely learned to watch what I said more closely," my friend told me.

It's not that I often don't have the urge to complain out loud while my toddler is in the room. It's just that I can't trust my toddler to keep her trap shut. I guess I'll have to keep mine shut instead.

Thems the Breaks

Toddlers are like jujitsu masters—continually kicking, hitting and head butting. It's unintentional, but that doesn't make it hurt any less. And it may be a blessing in disguise—if you've always wanted a nose job.

The first time my daughter almost broke my nose she was just a newborn. At least she was the cause of my almost nose break. I was so sleep deprived, thanks to her all-night wail fests, that I walked straight into a wall.

Now I'm getting more sleep, and I'm starting to think it may just be my nose that's the problem, not sleep deprivation.

My nose seems to be the one part of my body that my toddler always head butts, kicks with her bare feet or, even worse, kicks with her clunky shoes on.

My nose is either bigger than I thought—and I've always thought my nose was too big—or it's just an unfortunate coincidence that it's the one part of my body that is always getting in the way of her head/feet/fists. At least once a week my daughter head butts me in the nose, kicks me in the nose or smacks me in the nose.

I'm neither here nor there when it comes to plastic surgery. If you want a nose job, that's up to you and I'm not going to judge you. Actually, I've always wanted a nose job, but I've never been courageous enough to go through with it. Somehow, it just seems easier to convince myself that my nose gives me "character." Plus, I'm scared to go under the knife and mostly, save for Ashley Simpson, nose jobs don't make the person look prettier or better.

I'd probably be the type of person to get a nose job and look worse. So I'm not taking any chances.

But I'm pretty convinced that if things keep up the way they are now, I will be forced to have one.

The other day the Fiancé came home from work and I was sitting on the couch with an ice pack on my nose.

"Head butt?" he asked.

"Yup," I moaned.

"Painful?" he asked.

"Yup," I moaned.

I can't tell you how many times, since my baby turned into a toddler, that I've tasted blood in my mouth, or thought that some of my teeth had been knocked out.

The Fiancé may have it worse. The look on his face when the toddler kicks him in the nuts is priceless. And usually, she's just trying to jump on his lap, or climb over him.

Like my nose, his groin is the one place she always seems to jump on and kick. (I'm sorry, but it's always kind of funny when that happens. I'm sure this is mostly because I'm a girl and can't feel his pain—just like he can't imagine PMS or carrying around a baby for nine months.)

So frequent are these bumps and bruises that I barely get any sympathy anymore, when I scream, "I taste blood! I taste blood!"

What's worse is that you can't even scream as loud as you want to when the incident occurs. This is because you've just been playing tickling games with your toddler and she's having the best time ever. And suddenly the game must stop because there are tears in your eyes, you're checking to see if your nose is crooked and wondering if you're going to have two black eyes in the morning. You can't scare your toddler by screaming, "You hurt me!" Besides, you're already screaming, "I taste blood! I taste blood!"

Plus, it's not like she *meant* to hurt you. Toddlers just don't seem to have coordination. Either that, or like I've said, my nose is really, really big.

Yes, it's all fun and games until someone needs a nose job. Isn't that how the saying goes?

Mean Cinderella and Bad Santa

These are the hired costume-wearing characters at birthday parties or other child-friendly events who'd rather be out in the alleyway, smoking a butt and downing a bottle of red.

I know. You're asking, how can Cinderella, the princess of all princesses, be mean? She is beautiful and blonde, and has clear blue eyes and nice pink lips, and she gets to go to a ball and meet Prince Charming and wear cool glass slippers.

What the hell does Cinderella have to be grumpy about?

Well, I met Cinderella and she was *very* grumpy. She was as cranky as a pack-a-day smoker who had quit two days ago.

I met this Mean Cinderella at a 4-year-old's birthday party.

There are good birthday parties and there are bad birthday parties, and before every one you attend, you wonder what you're heading into. "Oh god," you think, "this had better be a good birthday party." When I first walked into the rented room at the community center, I thought, "Okay, this is going to be painful." The room was completely empty, aside from a table with pretzels and mini carrots.

I wondered, "Did this mother have a *plan* for this birthday party? Or are all the kids just supposed to run around for two hours?" I also thought, "This is going to be the longest two hours of my life."

But, then, Cinderella swept into the room. This was fantastic, I thought! This *was* going to be a good birthday party after all. The parents of the birthday girl had hired someone to dress up like Cinderella and play games with the toddlers.

My toddler, who is obsessed with all things princess, adores Cinderella.

Cinderella was dressed in her sweeping blue ball gown. Her blond hair was in an up-do.

My daughter was so excited, she started to yell out, "I never met Cinderella before! I never met her before!" as she jumped up and down like she had to pee. My toddler actually believed this Cinderella came right from the ball. *And was real.*

I immediately noticed the very large tattoo on Cinderella's left boob.

Her costume didn't exactly fit so well. She was definitely showing more boob than any other Cinderella I've seen in the movies or coloring books.

Okay, I thought, so she was a former-biker-turned-Cinderella. Hey, we all need day jobs right? We all have histories. We've all done things we regret.

And maybe in a previous life—before she was working at kids' birthday parties dressed as a Disney character—she was a biker chick or tattoo artist.

Big deal. Cinderella had a tattoo on her boob.

The kids were too caught up with having Cinderella there to notice her tattoo anyway. So why should I care?

But that wasn't the worst of it. Cinderella did not just have a tattoo on her breast. Cinderella actually made two children cry.

It all started because the toddlers were playing Cinderella Bingo. Now, personally—and I'm sure most parents of 2-, 3- and 4-year-olds would agree—I think that when you play bingo with toddlers, every child should win.

Fortunately, it did seem as if all the children got bingo at one point or another. Except for one little girl, who didn't quite understand the concept and just colored in all her squares.

Cinderella didn't like that. She refused to give this little girl a prize.

"That's not how you play bingo," Cinderella told this 3-year-old. "You don't get a prize. You didn't play right."

Which was totally ridiculous since the prizes were these mini plastic rings that probably cost, um, ten cents each. And it was mean. She was 3!

"Is she okay? What happened?" I asked the little girl's mother, as she tried to soothe her child.

"Oh, Cinderella made her cry."

Aside from the crying child part, it was actually pretty funny. Who knew Cinderella had it in her to be so cruel over Princess Bingo?

Even the crying child's mother was laughing. I mean, how often does friggin' Cinderella make children cry? I'm pretty sure—no, make that *I'm positive*—that it's not in Cinderella's job description to make children cry. Especially when she's been hired to make children happy at a birthday party.

The child eventually stopped crying, but only after her mother said, "Well, you have two choices. We can either stay at the birthday party—with Cinderella—or we can leave."

Her toddler, of course, wanted to stay. Not because of Cinderella, but because the cake hadn't been served yet.

After Princess Bingo, Cinderella pulled out her face-painting kit. My daughter, in her three years on this planet, has had her face painted about fifteen times, thanks to all the birthday parties and other child-friendly events we've attended.

Getting her face painted is the greatest joy *in her life*.

But this Cinderella was possibly the worst face painter in the entire history of children's face painters. (There went the theory that she was a former tattoo artist. Cinderella had no artistic talent.)

She basically painted three polka dots on the kids' faces and said, "Voila! You're a tiger!" "You're a bear." "You're a butterfly."

My daughter is shy, so I had to walk with her to Cinderella and say, "Rowan, tell Cinderella what you want on your face."

Because my daughter can sometimes be strange, she asked Cinderella to paint a pony.

Okay, granted, even if you were the most talented face painter in the world, it would be hard to paint a pony on a toddler's face, which is the size of a grapefruit.

But then Cinderella almost made *me* cry. She looked at me and said, "Well, I can't paint a pony on her entire face. I guess I could try just one cheek."

Cinderella didn't say this kindly. She was actually very rude about it, as if a toddler asking for a pony on her face was the most ridiculous request on the entire planet. I wondered if this Cinderella had ever spent time with a toddler before.

It was all I could do to stop myself from saying, "Cinderella! I've supported you by buying magazines about Cinderella, a ton of Cinderella costumes and a ton of Cinderella DVDs. Now paint a fucking pony on my child's face, or at least go through the motions of pretending to paint a fucking pony on her face! And stop complaining!"

I wanted to ask her if she had just quit smoking.

But I just looked at Cinderella sternly, and said, "Please try to paint a pony."

Cinderella painted something on my daughter's cheek. She said it was a pony, but mostly it looked like a big blob of brown paint.

Thankfully, my daughter is only a toddler. She was happy with the blob of brown paint.

Things continued to go downhill from there. Cinderella got quite bitchy with some of the children. "I'm only here for another couple of minutes, so I'll have to be fast," she said, although there were still a number of kids in line.

This led to an unusually high number of kids with red paint blotches on their cheeks. Cinderella meant business. She was only being paid for an hour and a half of her time and she was not going to spend one minute longer than she was supposed to at the birthday party.

Once Cinderella left, the party's entire vibe changed.

Frankly, all of us adults were a little petrified of this Cinderella. We didn't want to piss this Cinderella off. She was clearly in a bad mood the second she walked in, and hanging around screaming children who didn't understand the concept of Princess Bingo and who wanted ponies painted on their faces didn't help her mood any.

The rule of thumb in the hired dress-up character world is "buyer beware." You hire someone to come to your kid's birthday party dressed in character and you never know, aside from the costume, what you'll get.

Unfortunately, bad dress-up characters seem to far outweigh the good. You actually find yourself sucking up to clowns, just so they don't take out their bad moods on your child.

One of my friends told me about the time she hired a Santa Claus to entertain the children at a Christmas brunch. The first thing this Santa did upon walking in was demand a stiff alcoholic beverage.

"We were like, 'No! You are here to entertain the kids. You can't drink,'" my friend told me.

Another friend hired a Spider-Man for her son's party. "This Spider-Man showed up in full costume, but he was about 85 years old," she told me. "And the first thing he did when he arrived was tell the children, 'Okay, Spider-Man is very tired today. Spider-Man was out until 4 a.m.' He was clearly hungover!"

And, then, less than a year later, this mother hired him back! He dressed up as Superman for her other son's party. (I guess we should be happy he was still alive . . . and not in rehab.)

"I can't believe you hired him back!" I told her.

"Well, it's just easy. He knows where I live already," was her answer.

And then there was the "balloon making" clown at another birthday party. I put "balloon making" in quotes, because the "balloon making" clown made only balloons that resembled one of two things: two breasts with nipples or a penis with balls. The clown told the kids they were a "special breed of dogs."

Luckily, toddlers aren't that smart.

I guess the moral is that parents need to do background checks when hiring a dress-up character for a child's birthday party.

No one, after all, should be scared of Cinderella or a Bad Santa. Especially adults.

Part IX
Things I Should Probably Keep to Myself

Mommy: I love you, Jaina.
Jaina: I know.

Jaina, 16 months, daughter of Jeanet Moore

The Play Disaster

Play dates can go horribly wrong, ending up more like, "play don'ts." Sometimes, a "friend" will traumatize your child (and, more importantly, you) to the point where you think you will never again invite another toddler over, even if that means your child will lead a lonely, friendless life.

Eventually, all parents must do the "play date."

You may, for the first two years of your child's life, have somehow gotten out of the whole play date thing, but there will come a time when your toddler asks for a friend to "come to my house."

I spent the first two years of my baby's life not doing play dates. This was mostly because I'd realized that children under 2 don't really know how to play together anyway. I got together with friends and their children, but I refused to call these get-togethers "play dates."

Our kids just did their own thing, in their own corners.

But when your toddler is old enough to say, "Mommy, I want Sky to come to my house and play with my toys," you can't say, "No." And not just because you can't quickly think of a good excuse to get out of it. Even if you could think of a good excuse, you can't say "No" forever.

You will eventually have to invite Sky over.

So you e-mail Sky's mother because Sky is your daughter's best friend at pre-school and you do want your daughter to have friends. You go out and buy new finger paints and crayons and make arrangements with Sky's mother, who will drop off Sky at your house at 12:30 and pick her up at 3:30 p.m. You have mini-panic attacks because you can barely keep your own child entertained for three hours, let alone someone else's child.

And then, you think, maybe—just maybe—they can entertain *each other* for three hours and you won't have to do a thing. Maybe, you think, this play date won't turn out so bad after all.

But this will not be the case.

Your doorbell rings at exactly 12:30 p.m. and Sky comes in and her mother says "Hi" and that she's got to run to do errands. You're actually jealous of Sky's mother because she gets to do *errands*, even though you think, in the back of your mind, that Sky's mother is probably going to get a manicure, or home to take a nap.

You kind of want to leave with her, but you're the one who invited Sky over. *You agreed to this. You made the call.* You made your bed and now you have to sleep in it. You made this play date and now you must play.

You head downstairs to the playroom with your daughter and Sky and ask if they want to finger paint. They yell, "Yes!" and you think, "Alright, this might turn out okay." This will not be the case.

Sky, who you realize almost immediately is a bossy little thing ("I want that one now!") starts demanding the yellow paint, even though your daughter wants it too. The first fight starts two minutes after Sky's arrival. You are torn. You love your daughter a billion times more than you love this Sky—in fact, you don't even like this Sky all that much—but Sky is a guest, a guest you invited, and is also supposedly your daughter's "bestie." You must make Sky happy, even if it means sacrificing the happiness of your own child.

And then, just as you sort out the yellow paint issue, Sky starts screaming bloody murder for no apparent reason, and your daughter's face looks as frightened as it has ever looked, and you want to hug your daughter but you must calm down Sky first. Disaster momentarily averted. The kids move on from finger painting after fifteen minutes.

You realize that Sky's mother isn't coming to pick her up for another two hours and forty-five minutes and you think, "If I had the choice to watch paint dry for the next two hours and forty-five minutes or do this, I would choose watching paint dry."

You let the kids play with the millions of toys you have collected in your playroom. You realize that two toddlers don't make twice the mess as one. Two toddlers make ten times the mess as one.

They argue because Sky wants to play toy trains and your daughter wants to play in the tent, but finally they decide they want to dress up as princesses.

Luckily, you have two princess costumes, but Sky demands to wear the pink one. The pink princess costume is your daughter's favorite and you try to convince Sky that the purple princess costume is gorgeous. But Sky is stubborn and starts screaming and you start to think that your kid is amazing because she rarely throws temper tantrums like Sky.

But, again, you have to tell your daughter (whom you really just want to hug, because she's looking scared again) that Sky is the guest. You think to yourself, "It's only another two hours and thirty minutes of my life."

Your child is stuck with the purple princess dress while bossy Sky wears the pink one.

For the next hour, you watch Sky boss your child around and you don't really mind (but you do) because your child seems happy enough to listen to what Sky tells her. You make a mental note to tell your daughter, after Sky leaves, that she doesn't have to do everything Sky says.

And then you realize that it's time for snack. Their blood sugar may be getting low and you definitely don't want Sky going off again.

You feel a headache coming on.

Sky demands cucumbers, which luckily you have and she insists that they be cut up in squares. You do what Sky says because she is, after all, the guest. And, also, you admit, you're kind of pet-rified of this 3-year-old.

You pop two Advil.

Then Sky has another meltdown. She doesn't want to watch the DVD your daughter wants to watch so she screams and screams and screams. But, again, she's the guest and you let her pick.

Then Sky tells you she has to go to the bathroom, and you take her there and she tells you she doesn't need your help and you say, "You need my help. You're wearing a big princess dress and it will end up in the toilet if I don't help you," and then you think, "I can't believe I'm wiping someone else's kid."

Finally, you look at your watch and tell Sky she has to start getting ready to leave. Her mother is coming in five minutes and she must get on her coat and shoes.

Sky tells you she doesn't want to leave and you say (in a voice that's a little more desperate than you'd like), "You have to leave!" And then you add, "Because your mother misses you," so you don't sound like a royal bitch.

Sky's mother arrives right on time—thank the friggin' lord—and you're trying to see if her nails are sporting a new coat of pol-ish. Her hands, you notice, are sheepishly behind her back.

Sky's mother asks, "So how was she?"

You debate telling her that Sky was a nightmare and threw 300 temper tantrums and fought with your child over everything and that you have a migraine and that she is never invited back. But you don't know Sky's mother that well. All you know for sure is that Sky is now getting out of your house. And that's all that matters.

So you simply say, "She was great! They had a great time! She can come back anytime she wants!" Because telling a mother that her child is the Devil, after she asks how she was, would be akin to saying, "Yeah, it looks like you've gained a few," after someone asks if they look fat.

You can't be *honest*.

Sky's mother thanks you and you think she should also send flowers for the hell you've been through—the hell she will never know about because you are too much of a coward to tell her the truth.

A friend of mine was also naive in thinking that her first play date experience would be a good one. She was excited to be having another toddler over. She thought it would be good for her son.

My friend made the two kids macaroni and cheese for lunch. When she asked her little guest if he'd like a fork, the boy answered "No."

She assumed he wanted a spoon instead. "No," the boy told her. "I don't need anything." He then proceeded to shove the macaroni and cheese into his mouth with his hands. The macaroni and cheese was all over his face, in his hair and all over the floor, which my friend had to clean up.

Even her 3-year-old said, "That's gross." And you know when a 3-year-old—who thinks boogers are fun—considers something gross, it must really be gross.

"I kept wondering if he was raised in the woods," my friend told me. "He's never coming back."

Another friend says it's even worse when a friend's child is the nightmare. "I feel bad because she's a good friend of mine, but her son is a terror. He never picks anything up. He destroys everything. But I can't not have him come over."

As toddlers get older, play dates get meaner. Or so I understand from a friend who has raised three toddlers.

"One girl came over and she was evil. She kept saying, 'Your house is so small,' and, 'I'm bored,' and, 'There's nothing to do here,' over and over. It always ended in tears," she said.

Another mom was going through a home renovation at the time of the play date. "This girl came over and kept saying, 'Your house is scary. I want to go home. Your house is scary!' The next day at school, my daughter asked this girl if she wanted to come over and play again. The girl said, 'No! Your house is scary!' and that made my daughter cry. She was very hurt. That was painful."

No matter how horribly you think the play date went, your toddler's reaction will likely surprise you. A few hours after the Sky debacle, for example, my daughter said, "Mom, can Sky come to my house again to play?"

And you will say, "Of course!" while thinking, "Not a chance in hell," and, "Don't you remember that she made you cry?" But you will say "Of course" because it will buy you time to think of all the reasons Sky can't come over. You may even consider moving to get out of having Sky come over again.

You will wait a few weeks, all the while wondering if there's such a condition as Post-Traumatic Play Date Stress Syndrome. You keep waking up in the middle of the night, gasping for air, and thinking about Sky.

But in the end, you'll cave. In the end—because you love your daughter, who loves Sky—you will go through this hell again. You'll just wait a few weeks until you recover.

Nosy Mothers

We all know them, these mothers who will not mind their own business, who seem to care way too much about you and your toddler. You may find yourself biting your tongue to keep from saying, "It's none of your freakin' beeswax."

Nosy Mothers drive me nuts. Nosy Mothers ask you things like, "So, what classes have you signed your child up for?" and you know they're not asking because they're being friendly.

Nosy mothers have a certain look in their eyes and a certain edge to their voice. You know they're asking about your child's classes just because they are competitive and don't want their own toddler missing out on something. Nosy Mothers also ask things like, "So does your child know the different colors?" just to make sure your toddler, god forbid, doesn't know the colors of the rainbow before theirs.

The *worst* kind of Nosy Mother is the one who dares to question your mothering ability. Without actually saying to your face, "You suck as a mother," they make it clear that's exactly what they think about you.

I had an incident with a Nosy Mother when my toddler first started pre-school.

My daughter had caught a bad cold and I didn't send her to pre-school for two days. Near the end of her cold run, she got a cough. It wasn't serious. She didn't have a fever. Her energy was high. I sent her back to school.

After school, when I went to pick her up, this Nosy Mother said to me, "I heard that your daughter had a bad cold and wasn't in school for the past couple of days." She didn't say this with concern.

I mean, she was concerned—just not for my child. She was concerned that I had sent her to school with a cold her child might catch.

"Oh, she did. But she's better now," I told her.

Of course—because of Murphy's Law of Parenting—my child started coughing just at this moment.

"It seems like she still has a cough," this mother said to me.

"Oh, no. She's fine. She wasn't coughing at all this morning."

It was true. She hadn't been.

My daughter can cough on cue. She's learned that whenever she coughs, we all make a big deal over it and ask her, "Are you okay? Do you feel okay?"

When her friend caught an eye infection, and her mother bought her a lollipop, my toddler screamed, "I want an eye infection, too!"

Anyway, the next morning my daughter was in a chipper mood. She didn't even fake a cough just for sympathy.

I dropped her off at school. "I heard her coughing at school yesterday after you left and it was bad," the Nosy Mother said to me again, this time right in front of the teacher.

"I know. We were talking, remember?" I told her.

I felt like she had just told on me after I'd cheated on a test or something.

"No, she's fine," I said.

Twenty minutes later I got a phone call from the school.

"Rowan doesn't seem to be herself. She seems tired. She's coughing a lot," the teacher said. "Can you come pick her up?"

I knew—in my gut—it was all because of the Nosy Mother.

Why did this mother care so much? Trust me, no one cares about my daughter more than I do. What kind of mother did she think I was?

I hasten to add that I actually didn't have to send my toddler to school. At the time, I had a full-time nanny. I didn't have to send my toddler anywhere.

I drove back and picked up my daughter, who seemed more than fine. She seemed happy.

I wanted to say to this teacher, "Of course she seemed tired. She doesn't like to go to bed. She didn't get enough sleep."

And if—if—she coughed, it was only to get sympathy, and why can't you tell a fake cough from a real cough? What kind of teacher are you?

I was so angry at this Nosy Mother that I actually took my daughter to the doctor and told her that she was sent home from school.

The doctor said she was just fine. And she is a professional.

The next day I drove her back to school and said to the teacher, "I took her to the doctor and she's fine!" meaning, "Don't be calling me in twenty minutes just when I arrive home because another mother told on me."

Some mothers—usually nosy ones—seem to like their kids to live in a bubble. I'm not saying it's right to send your child to school or play group or daycare when they're sick with a fever or the flu or a really bad cold.

At the same times, toddlers get colds. All the time. If I were to keep my toddler home every time she had a bad cold, she wouldn't leave the house between October and July.

Generally, I'm not a Nosy Mother. Generally.

Once at summer camp a toddler who looked as if she had impetigo or a really bad cold sore was dropped off.

I thought to myself, "Gross!" and also, "What kind of mother sends her kid to camp with a big honking cold sore?"

Now, I would never say this to the mother. Instead, I asked the girl what happened to her face.

"I fell off the slide," she answered. So maybe it wasn't impetigo, or a cold sore. Maybe this kid really did fall off a slide. (The cynic in me wonders if her mother spent two hours before dropping her off at camp, saying, "You fell off a slide. This is not contagious. You fell off a slide. This is not contagious. If anyone asks, you fell off a slide. What happened? Yes, you fell off a slide.")

The point is, your toddler is going to get a cold, or pinkeye, or impetigo or lice. If not from my toddler, then from someone else's.

So, Nosy Mothers, suck it up and quit telling on the rest of us. We're all in the same leaky boat.

Supermodel Moms

There are women out there who, like supermodels, were put on this earth for no other reason than to torture you. They wear white, look great and make mothering seem effortless. And horror of all horrors, they are skinny, too. Bitches.

Not long ago, I had a mortifying mothering moment when a Super Mom, who was at my house for a play date, saw all the toys from McDonald's Happy Meals in one of my toddler's toy chests.

I refuse to count all these Happy Meal toys for fear of really comprehending just how many times, in the three years my toddler has been on earth, I've taken her to the fast food joint. (It's like how I refuse to do the math on how much money I spend at Starbucks every year, thanks to my daily non-fat grande latte addiction.)

I just knew we had a shitload of Happy Meal toys.

"Oh, I see your daughter goes to McDonald's," she said, eyeing the treasure trove of toys. "I've only taken Sam once. I'm really strict about junk food. I don't allow it. We try to be as organic as possible. Plus, she doesn't like junk food. She prefers vegetables."

I changed the subject by asking Super Mom where she got her fabulous (unstained, tucked in, white) sweater.

"Paris," she told me. "We go a few times a year to shop. Sam loves it. She can understand French!"

Newsflash: there are mothers out there who have been put on this planet to make you feel like a bad mother (and a pathetic excuse for a woman).

Over coffee the other day, one of my best mother friends told me—with glee in her voice—that another mother had come up to her at school and said, "I just want to tell you that you always look so calm and collected."

My friend was thrilled with this compliment. It was as if it was the nicest compliment she had ever received in her entire life. And why shouldn't she be thrilled? It practically *is* the nicest compliment I've ever heard. Oh, to be thought of as "calm" and "collected." I could only dream!

There's this one mother at my child's pre-school who makes me feel like shit even if I see her from way down the hallway. In fact, I don't even have to see this Super Mom. If I smell her expensive perfume lingering in the elevator, I feel like shit.

I just don't understand how, at 8:35 a.m., this mother can be dressed in a Chanel suit and Dolce & Gabanna boots—with full makeup, her hair up as if she's going to a ball—while I'm wearing an extra large sweater over my pajama top, ripped jeans and no bra. Oh, and to add insult to injury, this Super Mom is stick-thin too.

My toddler shows up to pre-school with toothpaste on her face, looking like a mop-top. If I'm lucky, one ponytail is still in. Super Mom's toddler comes to school looking like she just came from the salon.

I often wonder what Super Mom thinks of me. Now, you might ask, why do I care what other mothers think of me—a pajama-wearing-did-I-brush-my-teeth-this-morning-I-can't-remember mother?

Well, I'm older and wiser, yes, and I no longer bow down to peer pressure, but I'm still *female*, for god's sake. And women have this amazing ability to make other women second-guess how they look. They make you wonder whether you're a good mother. They make you want to run a comb through your hair.

No matter how comfortable you are in your own skin, another woman can make you feel inadequate. It's like how I know I'm short. But knowing it doesn't make it any easier to accept—

especially when tall, skinny, supermodel-types are strutting about all around me.

Being short bugs me. Supermodels bug me. Super Moms bug me.

I like to think that these Super Moms—after they tell you about their homemade, organic, trans-fat-free, television-free homes, while dressed in designer clothes with no rips or stains that they bought on their vacations to Italy—are all sobbing at home in their beds every night.

I know this is mean. But I don't care.

Super Moms make me feel bad because I allow my toddler to watch television while eating meals. I show up to school in pajamas not just to drop off my toddler but also (sometimes) to pick her up—four hours later. I take my toddler to McDonald's. Often. I do not look on boxes for "trans-fat free" labels.

There's another Super Mom at school—and it's unfortunate because she is so friendly it's impossible to hate her—who drops off and picks up her toddler every single day.

Which would be fine if she didn't also bring along her two other kids (she's one of those, "I have three kids under the age of 3" mothers). These kids are *never* crying or even whining.

And I haven't once seen this Super Mom wearing anything looking even remotely like pajamas. Sometimes I see her standing there, waiting for her kids to come out. She looks so perfect and relaxed, I want to throw a stone at her—just to make sure she's not a cutout poster for a spa.

I find it hard enough to get out the door with one child *and* my hair brushed, so I wonder how she does it with three kids, while still managing to look so put together and calm.

Then there are the rich mothers. Disgustingly rich mothers, whose children have $50,000 parties to celebrate turning 2.

I'm okay with that. If you're rich, great. If you're super, disgustingly rich, great. Lucky you. Invite me to your kid's party.

But these mothers also make me feel bad. It shouldn't matter how much money one has. I know this, logically. But, still, they make me feel bad. One mother at my daughter's pre-school is filthy rich. (And again, she's super nice, so I can't hate her. Why can't these Rich Super Moms be at least a tad bitchy?) My daughter has decided that Rich Super Mom's daughter is her best friend. Her daughter is sweet and nice (and you can't hate a 3-year-old for having a better wardrobe than you). I should be happy, right?

But here's the thing. My daughter has this one pair of shoes that I call her "special" shoes. It's not politically correct to say, I know, but these shoes are the fugliest shoes in the history of all shoes. The heels are thick, kind of like the equivalent of bottle-glass lenses on her feet. These "special" shoes are also super disgusting because my toddler loves them so much that she has worn them every day for months upon months, in the rain, in the mud. These shoes are an embarrassment to shoes everywhere.

We were picking our children up at school and Rich Super Mom and I were shooting the shit, me wondering if Rich Super Mom could tell I was too lazy to put on a bra, or could smell that I hadn't showered. I was also wondering, how was it possible this woman is a mother—when she looks so damn good all the time?

Our kids came out together holding hands. It was all very cute until I looked down at her daughter's feet only to see that she was wearing my daughter's disgusting muddy "special" shoes. I was mortified! My daughter, of course, was wearing Rich Super Kid's shiny black patent loafers that looked so clean I would lick them.

"Oh, I'll just put her in the car and I'll take the shoes off and give them right back to you," Rich Super Mom said.

"No it's okay," I said. "You can return them whenever. It's no problem," thinking, oh . . . my . . . god. Why does the richest kid in school—who actually has a pair of Prada shoes (yes, they do make them for kids)—have to be wearing my daughter's "special" shoes?

"No, no. It's no problem," Rich Super Mom told me.

I could tell she didn't want these "special" muddy shoes on her daughter's feet any more than I wanted them on my daughter's feet.

My friend has an even worse story. There's one mother who always makes her feel bad, because she's a Super Mom, super rich, super skinny and just plain super all around (all of us know at least one of these).

"Bitch!" I said about this Super Mom.

"I know," my friend said. "But I haven't even told you the story yet."

"Right. Go on," I said.

One night my friend was putting her two toddlers to bed and she ended up falling asleep with them in their room, all three of them on one of her sons' beds.

Her husband, meanwhile, was out on the driveway. So, when super rich, skinny, couture-dressed Super Mom and her husband happened by on an evening stroll (there goes my theory that Super Moms are at home sobbing), my friend's husband invited them in. My friend had just moved into the neighborhood and her husband wanted to give them the full tour.

And by full tour, I mean full tour—including the room in which my friend was sleeping with her two toddlers. "I had fallen asleep in one of my husband's t-shirts and this pair of sweatpants I've had for ten years. My socks didn't match," my friend told me. Her husband didn't tell her about this until the next morning.

I should also mention my friend drools when she sleeps. So there she was—shoved in a twin bed with her two toddlers, drooling with mismatched socks—while this Super Mom watched in all her Super Mom glory.

"I swear, I can't get it out of my mind that this woman saw me drooling," my friend moaned. "I just know she thinks that I'm the most disgusting woman ever."

The point is that Super Moms are everywhere. Even when you're asleep, they're there, watching.

The Party Circuit

You always wanted to be a Party Girl, but now you find yourself praying to god, "Please don't invite us!" The toddler birthday parties are never-ending. Once you're in the Party Circuit, you can never get out. Your weekends are booked until 2024.

I used to love invitations. Receiving one meant that I was wanted somewhere. It also meant that I would probably have a good time. (Pre-baby, I remember actually not minding a hangover. What else did I have to do the next day but work?)

Sometimes, in the pre-mother days, I would even get three different invitations for events on the same night! I would think it was thrilling to flitter around town attending three parties in one evening.

Was I really once so obnoxious that I would be, like, "Got to run. Another party!" Of course, that was back then, before I had a baby, when I had something called "energy."

I don't have "energy" anymore.

I barely have the "energy" to open an invitation. Quite seriously. The mere thought of ripping open an envelope drains me. That's because I hate invitations now. But I'm not talking about invitations to friend's parties or cool bar openings. I'm talking about children's birthday party invitations.

At my daughter's pre-school, there's a rule: if you have a birthday party, you must invite all the children in the class. On paper, this sounds reasonable. Especially if your child is the class loser. (As, I'll admit, I sometimes think mine possibly is. Okay, I shouldn't say that. She's just shy.) Apparently, it's the politically correct thing to do, inviting all the kids in the class.

It's also the biggest pain in the ass.

Not only do you have to invite all the kids to *your* toddler's birthday party, but also you will get invited to everyone else's toddlers' birthday parties. (Not to mention all your other friends, outside school, who have toddlers whose birthday parties you will also be invited to.)

In the next two weeks, I have three kids' birthdays to attend with my toddler. I've been to two others in the last two weeks. One recent Saturday we had two parties in the same day! These days, all my weekends—which used to be about sleeping in, going out for brunch and taking afternoon naps—are consumed by attending toddler birthday parties and working my days around these birthday parties.

My entire *week*, these days, seems to be spent going to and from toy stores to buy gifts for all these damn birthday parties and asking myself, "Did I RSVP?"

Each day, when I pick up my child from pre-school, what I dread most is not that she'll be cranky and hungry (which she usually is). No, what I dread most is the little cubbyhole in her classroom with her name on it.

The little cubbyhole is where letters from the principal are stashed, and where the artwork your child has done in class that day is kept for you to take home. It is also where parents leave birthday invitations. I dread that cubbyhole as much as I dread going to the dentist (and I dread the dentist so much I haven't been in three years).

It's not because I don't like to see my toddler's finger paintings—I do. I dread the cubbyhole because I know, chances are, there will be a birthday invitation there. And that invitation means another weekend ruined and another last-minute race to a store to buy a gift for the birthday girl or boy.

You know how people always complain—except the bride and

groom—about weddings on long weekends? I am one of those peo-ple now, except for me, every weekend seems like a ruined long weekend. And it's all thanks to the never-ending toddler birthday parties.

I am not afraid to admit it: When I see another little envelope with my daughter's name written on the outside, I think to myself, "Oh, no. Not again! Crap!"

Once your toddler starts making friends, or goes to school, you become part of what I call the Birthday Party Circuit. And—like the clueless characters in a horror movie who check into a hotel for a romantic mini-vacation, only to find that the friendly neigh-borhood psychopath has booked into the room next door—you can't escape. Once you're in the Party Circuit, you can never get out. It's like the friggin' Hotel California.

"Come on, Rebecca, you know all the hot parties. You're in loop. What parties are going on?" a friend asked me one late Saturday afternoon.

"Oh, I'm in a party loop, all right. But it's not the type of loop you're looking for," I told him.

"What?" asked my single, child-free, guy friend.

"God, I can barely talk. I have baby birthday brain," I moaned to him.

"Is that some kind of new drug?" he asked.

"No, you idiot! It's the feeling of a pounding headache because you just spent three hours with thirty kids. Which is what I did this afternoon. I'm not going out tonight," I told him. (Don't even ask me what baby birthday brain felt like after the party where sixty toddlers were invited.)

As far as I can tell, the only thing toddler birthday parties *are* good for is killing two hours of a day, and scratching one meal off the list of things you have to cook for your child.

Even so, I'm not sure toddlers get the concept of birthday

parties. (Okay, I know they don't, because at every birthday party we attend as guests, my daughter wants to sit in front of the cake and blow out the candles.) Which is a shame since you usually have to drive halfway across the world to get to the damn things! Why is it always such a pain in the ass to get to these community centers or gyms?

And, of course, it's either a venue you've never gone to before (and are not sure you'll find), or it's a place you've been a million times before (and so you're bound to be bored). I'm not sure what's more nerve wracking: having to find a new place and be on time, or having to go to the same birthday venue for the 102nd time.

Plus, some weird mothering instinct does kick in before these things. You think because it is a birthday party, that maybe you should dress your child a bit better than usual. Which just adds to the stress. You try so hard to make your child look "presentable," but by the time you arrive she has gummy bears stuck in her hair and she's spilled her apple juice all over herself.

All I can say is that if you're still at the stage where you enjoy getting birthday invitations, cherish it. There will come a time—probably very soon—when you won't enjoy being in the Party Circuit anymore.

One of my friends and I were moaning about birthday invitations we'd both received for a Saturday afternoon. They were for different parties, but they both happened to be at swimming pools.

"Will you be going to yours?" I asked my friend.

"No. I think we might just be out of town that weekend," she said. "At least that's what I'm going to say."

My friend and I both hate swimming parties, because you have to change your child, and shower her, and dry her hair, and it's all a little too much hassle for a 2-year-old (and her mother) to go through.

"Are you going to go to yours?" my friend asked me.

"Definitely not. We'll also be, um . . . maybe we'll have lost the invitation," I told her.

"Lost the invitation," is such a sad excuse.

"This is why you buy a cottage," my friend, the mother of twins, told me after I moaned that I had yet another birthday party to attend on the same weekend.

"What?" I asked, not understanding.

"We bought a cottage because of all the birthday invitations," she said. "Now, when we get invitations, we just say that we're going to the cottage for the weekend."

Suddenly it clicked. Maybe *this* is why families have cottages. It's not to enjoy the great outdoors or the boat rides, to barbecue hamburgers and hotdogs, to breathe the clean air or listen to the peaceful sound of loons.

It's simply to get out of going to birthday parties. It's brilliant!

If you do the math about how many birthday presents you'll buy in your child's lifetime, it may make financial sense to shell out for a down payment on a cottage instead.

In fact, I decided to use "going to the cottage" as my new excuse for getting out of some of these birthday parties. That is until one mother apologized to me at school a couple of weeks after my daughter's birthday. "Sorry we couldn't make it. We were at the cottage," she told me.

Ri-ight . . .

I'm on to you, woman. I'm on to you.

The Blame Game

One of the benefits of having a toddler who doesn't yet speak in full sentences is that you can use her as an excuse. They're the perfect alibis.

There are many unintentional bonuses to having children. Children, for one, offer a great excuse to cancel plans at the last minute. This is called "Pulling Out the Kid Card."

There have been a handful of times that I've pulled out the kid card to get out of going out for dinner. When I made the plans, I didn't realize it was the season finale of my favorite television show. As if I'm going out after dedicating thirty-nine hours, over three months, to watching *So You Think You Can Dance*. As if!

You know the whole, "I think my daughter is coming down with the flu. She feels a bit feverish. I don't think I'll be able to make it," routine? That's Pulling Out the Kid Card.

Friends can't argue with you if you're staying home with your sick, feverish child (even if you are lying). If they don't understand, and say something like, "Can't you just leave her for an hour? I'm sure she'll be fine," they aren't human (even if you are lying).

Using your toddler as an excuse is also easier than coming up with a more self-centered reason for bailing. You don't have to go through the whole act of pretending to sound nasally or forcing a cough.

I have also used the "I can't get a baby-sitter" excuse when invited to some event I'd rather poke my eyes out than attend. Saying, "Sorry, I don't have a baby-sitter," is a lot less painful, and a heck of a lot easier, than poking one's eye out.

The baby-sitter excuse is handy for early exits, as well. "The baby-sitter needs to be home by 11 p.m." works like a charm when I'm stuck at some event that, again, I'd rather poke my eye out than stay at one minute longer.

I know that other parents use their kids as excuses. I know it. I mean, I get the, "I think my son's coming down with something," excuse.

I don't have proof that these friends are lying to me. But, if I do it, I figure other parents do it and it's so strange when people just have to cancel on the exact night that *American Idol* or *Grey's Anatomy* ends.

It doesn't really bother me. I'm probably exhausted anyway, and grateful that you're canceling.

Another unintentional benefit of having a toddler is the Blame Game. You can blame a whole heck of a lot of things on toddlers—and not just when it comes to getting out of seeing a friend you're not in the mood to see, or getting out of your great aunt's (three times removed) 75th birthday brunch.

You can blame on your toddler the fact your pizza slice slid off your plate and onto the new carpet because you were also carrying a can of Diet Coke and a magazine and a chocolate bar at the same time. (Not that I've done this. Ahem.)

You can blame all stains on your toddler, like the coffee stain on the kitchen carpet. (Not that I've done this. Ahem.)

One of my friends always blames her gas on her toddler. It's sad, but true. (More sad, I suppose, is that my friend is so gassy that she has to blame it on her toddler.)

And sometimes things break. Like our remote control. It broke because our toddler threw it against a wall. Okay, I'm so lying. That was my fault. Or rather, the TiVo's fault for cutting off the last two minutes of my favorite show. But some things are better kept to yourself. Some things are better to blame on the toddler.

You can do this, though, only before they can speak and rat you out. "No, I didn't, Mommy. You did that! You're lying!" There's really only a small window of opportunity to pull out the kid card. Use it wisely.

Small Talk for Big People

As a parent, you'll find yourself in situations where you have to hang out with other parents. You'll have nothing to say to these people, but you'll be stuck with them for the next two hours. You'll wish it was appropriate to drink wine at an 11 a.m. birthday party, because it's much easier to make small talk when you're a tad tipsy.

You can't be antisocial when you're the mother of a toddler.

You will find yourself in situation after situation after situation after situation where you will be forced into a little thing called Small Talk. Which isn't that small a thing, it turns out. Mostly, this is because you can't be drunk. You can't even be tipsy. You also can't be the one mother hunched in a corner with her jacket still on during a birthday party, talking on her cellphone to her real friends. You don't want to be that mother because the other parents will think you're a bitch. Really, you're not a bitch. You just have nothing to say.

Or maybe you're trying to think of something pithy and interesting to say. Maybe, for the life of you, you can't think of a damn thing to say, which is why you're hunched in a corner praying that no one thinks you're a bitch, and that a friend will call you on your cell, hoping the other parents simply assume you're just really shy.

Parenting Small Talk is much worse than Office Small Talk during holiday parties. With Office Small Talk, you can at the very least gossip about co-workers or bitch about work or complain about how lame it is that the company didn't provide an open bar.

Most importantly, you can be drunk (even if you have to pay for those drinks), which means that even if you hate all your co-workers, you won't be tongue-tied.

You can't, however, be drunk at a birthday party for a 4-year-old, which takes place at 9:30 a.m. (I have been to one of those). And you certainly can't be drunk when you drop off your toddler at school at 8:30 a.m. (If you are, I suggest you get help immediately.)

Being drunk is a great way to get over the fear of Small Talk with people you don't really know. Everyone knows this. I'm the type of person who heads directly to the bar at a party, or who will meet a friend for a glass of wine at a bar before even attending the party. Most parties require Small Talk with people I don't know, and I like to be prepared.

I always thought I was pretty good at Small Talk—until I became a mother. I've been to many parties in the past decade with people I didn't really know after all. And, after half a glass of wine (I'm a lightweight), I'm quite comfortable asking how your relationship is going or how work is going or if you've thought about having children yet. I may even tell you that I don't like wearing underwear.

But when it comes to Parenting Small Talk, it just doesn't seem to get easier.

Don't get me wrong. I like almost all the mothers I see almost every weekend at birthday parties. I like all the parents I see while dropping off or picking up my toddler from school. The parents I sit around with watching my toddler in dance class seem perfectly nice.

It's just that I have nothing to say to them. Really. Even after all the birthday parties I've been to with these other parents, even after seeing them five days a week doing the pickup and drop-off, I still have a hard time doing the whole Small Talk thing.

How many times can you tell a mother how cute her child is? (A lot.)

How many times can you ask another mother if her toddler likes school? (A lot.)

How many times can you ask another mother where she bought her child's shoes? (A lot.)

I always wish that I could just say to these parents, "You know what? Let's all get together for drinks!"

I'm really fun when I'm tipsy! They'd know the real me! (And maybe I would learn more about them than their first names.) They wouldn't think that I have nothing to say and am the most boring person on the planet! I have a lot to say! I have really interesting things to say! I swear!

But you wouldn't know it from the way I Small Talk. Take this morning's fascinating conversation with a mother at my daughter's school, to whom I say "hello" every day. She was carrying both of her sons' knapsacks and their hockey equipment.

"Hi!" I said.

"Hi!" she said.

"How are you?" I asked.

"Good. How are you?" she asked.

"Good. Wow, you're carrying a lot of bags." I said.

"I know," she said.

"Okay, see you," I said.

"Bye," she said.

This kind of mind-blowing boring conversation would be fine, if it happened once a month. But it doesn't. It happens almost every day.

At birthday parties, which happen every weekend, the Small Talk goes like this.

"This is a great venue," I'll say.

"Yes, it is. The kids seem to love it," the mother will say.

"They do," I'll say.

"Yes, they really seem to love it," the mother will say again.

"Yes, they do," I'll say.

Or . . .

"I love cheesies," I'll say, hanging around the junk food table, stuffing my mouth.

"Me too," another mother will say.

"I can't stop eating these," I'll say.

"Me either," the mother will say.

And we'll stand around in an awkward silence, stuffing cheesies into our mouths.

You're actually grateful when it's time to sing "Happy Birthday" because at least you know what words have to come out of your mouth.

Many mothers I know have a difficult time with the Small Talk because they don't actually want to be friends with the other parents. Hey, I get that. We all already have our own friends.

But I'm not opposed to becoming friends with these parents. It's just, how can you become friends when all you do is Small Talk, and it's not even good Small Talk? How do you take it to the next level? What comes after, "I like cheesies," but before, "So are you divorced?" (I'm certainly not comfortable telling these parents that I don't wear underwear.)

Small Talk with teachers or daycare workers can also be painful.

A conversation, almost daily, with my toddler's teacher goes something like this.

"So how was she today?" I'll ask, when I pick her up.

"She was great! She's always perfect," her teacher will tell me.

This will piss me off.

Because what can I say to that except, "Good. Well, see you tomorrow."

"See you tomorrow," the teacher will say.

I honest to god sometimes wish my child would be the Bad Kid. I wish she'd get sent to the Time-out Chair. At least that way the Small Talk could turn into an actual conversation, with her teacher telling me about what she did wrong and why she ended up in the naughty chair. But, oh no, it's just my luck that I have a well-behaved child, at least at school. I have nothing to say to the teacher except, "See you tomorrow."

But it can get worse. Trust me. There are actually humans out there who are worse than parents or teachers on the Small Talk torture scale.

Toddlers.

Toddlers are the absolute worst. But if your friends have toddlers, you do have to make an effort to have conversations with them.

The other day, I was at my friend Victoria's house. She has two toddlers, both of whom I adore. Though the fact that I adore her children doesn't make it easier to talk to them.

Victoria's son had put a piece of salami on his head. He's 3, so this makes sense. Anyway, I was trying to have a conversation with him.

"I'm a salami head," he told me.

"Yes, you are! You are a salami head!" I said.

"I'm a salami head!" he said again.

"Yes, you are!" I said again.

And that's pretty much all I had to say to that. (Which, come to think of it, is still a more interesting Small Talk conversation than, "You're carrying a lot of bags!")

The only thing that makes me feel better about the fact I just don't know how to make Small Talk is that other parents don't seem to be very good at it either. It's not like any of them are asking my opinion on the war, or our government. They're telling me that they like my kid's shoes and asking if she enjoys school every time I see them.

Next skating lesson, I may just have to hide a flask. And pass it around.

Toddler-Offs

The new phase of Baby-Offs, when you realize that the parents who told you their babies were geniuses have now turned into parents who tell you their toddlers are geniuses.

I love the term Baby-Off. It explains competitive parenting to a T.

A Baby-Off is what happens when you are a new mother and you start talking to other new mothers, and you realize that you're not really having a discussion, shooting the shit or making small talk. Instead, you're listening to them tell you how great their babies are, how they sleep through the entire night, already have a 3.8 grade point average and have been accepted to Yale. And they're only 12 weeks old!

If you're not careful you can't help but get competitive yourself. You find yourself starting to say things like, "I just know from the shape of my daughter's legs she's going to be a prima ballerina," even though you have not a clue about bone structure and your baby spends eighteen hours a day sleeping in the car seat. The only thing you know is that some other mother just told you she's convinced her son is going to be a star hockey player, so you have to say something.

I always tried to get out of Baby-Offs. Mostly because I didn't have anything to show off. I'm not saying my baby was slow or anything (although it did take her a while to realize that the couch had an end and she couldn't just keep crawling off it without falling flat on her face or that if she didn't look in front of her when she walked she'd walk right into a wall). I'm just saying I never saw the point in saying, "Yes, I know, she's only 4 months old and she can speak!"

I've found myself in Baby-Off moments when parents have said to me, "She started speaking at six months!" Then I would actually see their baby, close up, in real life, only to hear, "Ga ga goo goo blah doink."

Fine, I thought. Whatever tickles your fancy. If you consider *Ga ga goo goo blah doink*, "speaking," then it's your prerogative to go around saying your 6-month-old blob speaks.

At one point, I thought that Baby-Offs were a phase, and that they would end when the babies grew up. That was idiotic. It's not a phase. It's an epidemic. Baby-Offs just morph into Toddler-Offs, and suddenly you find yourself listening to the mother of a toddler saying, "My child is in skating on Mondays, the Lego club on Tuesdays, French on Wednesdays, Mandarin classes on Thursdays and Science Club on Fridays. And he loves them all! All of his teachers think he's going to be a multilingual Olympic figure-skater who will win the Nobel Prize!"

I met a very nice mother at a park who told me her daughter takes karate. I think karate is a brilliant idea for toddlers. They'll know how to protect themselves, it's a form of exercise and they look so darn cute in their little karate outfits.

So I mentioned to one of my other mother friends that the mother I'd met had signed her daughter up for karate. I thought that we should sign our toddlers up for karate together. It turns out that my mother friend actually knows this mother I sometimes see at the park.

"I don't think we're allowed to sign them up so young," my friend told me.

"Why? That other girl is signed up. And she's younger than both our children," I said.

"Oh, her mother told me they made an exception for her because she was advanced," my mother friend told me.

"Advanced? Advanced at karate? But they just learned to run without tripping!" I exclaimed.

I see this supposedly "advanced" karate toddler at the park quite often. The kid is cute, I'll give her that. But I can't see her being some genius toddler karate master. She's, like, two feet tall and eats sand.

Maybe I'm just envious. Maybe I'm envious when I listen to other mothers of toddlers say, "Oh, she's just perfect. She goes to sleep at 7 p.m. sleeps through the night and then makes me break-fast in the morning."

I know that's pushing it. But when other mothers try to engage me in Toddler-Offs, that's what I hear. It doesn't matter what they are really saying.

Just like I hoped that Baby-Offs would stop, I hope that Toddler-Offs stop—and soon. But I realize this probably won't be the case. One of my writer friends, who's in his 40s, told me a story about how he went to a cocktail party with his mother (who is in her 70s) to honor a well-known writer. And by well known, I mean this writer is a household name.

My writer friend was mortified when his mother said to this author, "My son is an author, too!" so proudly and then said, "He's very talented! You should read some of his work."

I kind of thought it was sweet that his mother bragged about him. It was an Adult-Off!

I think that parents will always be super proud of their kids and that rather than wait for the Toddler-Off to stop, I'll have to start bragging more. My mother-in-law still says with glee, "My son is a lawyer! At a big law firm!"

So, here it goes: My toddler is only 3, but she got up this morning and vacuumed the house, took the dog out for a walk, folded all the laundry on her own and played quietly by herself for the next four hours. Then she did her multiple times table.

That's my story and I'm sticking to it.

Embarrass-Springs

You can't win. Either your toddler is having a Very Public Meltdown, or she's happily singing at the top of her lungs. Either way, everyone is staring.

I hate to say this, but my toddler sometimes embarrasses me.

It's one thing for her to have a Very Public Meltdown. That's sort of embarrassing but, really, it's more mortifying than anything else.

It's another thing entirely for her to be in a good mood when we're out in public. It does happen occasionally.

When my toddler is in a good mood, she likes to sing. Loudly. Proudly.

It's like that saying, "Dance as if no one is watching." I love that saying. But my daughter, when she's in a good mood, sings as if no one can hear. She sings so loudly, I swear, that my brother who lives on the outskirts of town could probably hear her.

"Apple, peaches, pears and plums. Tell me when your birthday comes! IS IT JANUARY, FEBRUARY, MARCH, APRIL, MAY, JUNE, JULY, OCTOBER?" she screamed out the other day while we were grocery shopping at Whole Foods.

Screaming and singing is almost the same thing in Toddler Land. There's no tone. There are just words. Words they scream.

I wasn't embarrassed that she forgot some of the months. I was embarrassed because she was singing as if no one could hear. But, boy, people could hear. They all turned to stare. But because she was singing as if no one could hear, she didn't notice all the stares. I did though. And I made that look like, "Kids! Aren't they cute? Can't live with them, can't live without them." It's a look I've come to perfect.

Before I became a parent, I had a male friend who had a young daughter. One day, I asked him what he had done. "I took my daughter on the subway," he said.

"Oh, that sounds like fun," I said.

"Actually," he said. "It's embarrassing to take her out."

I thought it was pretty rude that his own daughter embarrassed him and I told him so.

"She just talks to everybody," he moaned. "She talks to perfect strangers. Non-stop."

Now, my daughter doesn't talk to everybody. In fact, it's likely she will just plain ignore you if you ask her something.

But, oh, how she loves to sing. Loudly. Proudly.

Another day, I ran into a friend at a coffee shop. My daughter, unbelievably, was again in a good mood.

"Twinkle, twinkle, little star, HOW I WONDER WHERE YOU ARE. UP ABOVE THE WORLD SO BRIGHT. LIKE A DIAMOND IN THE SKY. Twinkle, TWINKLE, LITTLE STAR! HOW I WONDER WHERE YOU ARE." she screamed/sang.

I mean, yes, it sounds cute. For the first ten seconds or so. But when your daughter continues to sing, and your friend asks you, "Does she always sing like that?" as if your child is weird, it becomes a little embarrassing.

And it's not just singing. It's the talking, too. Toddlers don't have verbal editing like us adults.

We were in an elevator yesterday that was quite full. There were at least seven other people taking the ride with us when my daughter announced, "My booby hurts."

She said it loudly. Proudly.

Riding elevators, at the best of times, is an uncomfortable experience.

"MY BOOBY HURTS," she said louder, scratching her left nipple.

This four-floor elevator ride seemed to be taking forever. People were giggling. For everyone else, I suppose, it sounded sort of cute. I would have laughed too if it weren't my own toddler announcing that her "booby hurt." But I was embarrassed. Didn't she know not to talk about her breasts in public? Didn't she know she doesn't even have breasts?

"MY BOOBY IS SCRATCHY," she said. I scratched it, hoping the elevator ride would end. Please, dear god, let us get to the ground floor already.

People were laughing. And how could they not?

"When we get home can we put a Band-Aid on my booby?" she asked. I seriously felt myself blushing.

"Yes. We'll put a Band-Aid on," I said.

"We'll put a Band-Aid on my booby?" she asked.

"Yes!"

I had a similar reaction when we were on the street one day and she announced, "I have to pee-pee. PEE-PEE."

Okay, dear child, don't talk about your boobies or your urination in public.

But, soon enough, I know, my toddler will be embarrassed by me. One of my friends has a 4-year-old who is embarrassed when my friend picks her up from school wearing her glasses. Her kid will say, "My Mommy doesn't always wear glasses, you know."

"She's completely embarrassed by me sometimes," my friend says.

So I only have a year or so before the tables are turned and she's embarrassed by me. And it won't be because I'm singing as if no one can hear me. It'll just be because I'm me. Her mother.

Acknowledgments

I owe everything to my mother and father for not only being supportive and wonderful parents but for being even better as "Bubby" and "Zaida" to Rowan. So much love for S.J.C., a wonderful friend and father. Glenda and Dave are also perfect grandparents. We are so lucky to have them in our lives. My editor, Linda Pruessen, is not only a joy to work with and a fabulous editor, but a good friend now, too. Thanks to Jordan Fenn, who manages to keep up with the mayhem of children and work, all with a smile. My brothers and their wives and my nephews are always in my thoughts. My heroes remain: Ken Whyte, Dianne de Fenoyl, Jake Gold, Lorne London, Ron Johnson, Liza Cooperman, Sheri Segal, Mark Gollom, Ceri Marsh, Dana Fields, Carolynn Ross, Tessa Sproule, Helena, Nanny Mimi, Erica Ehm. Much thanks to Denise and the staff at The Bukowski Agency, and to Parmjit Parmar. And to all you mothers—especially those contributed "cute toddler" quotes—I bow down.